Faster, Cheaper, Better

Starting and Operating a Business in the Trades

Jack Borden

Faster, Cheaper, Better

Starting and Operating a Business in the Trades

Self-Counsel Press
(a division of)
International Self-Counsel Press Ltd.
USA   Canada

Self-Counsel Press acknowledges the financial support of the Government of Canada through the Canada Book Fund (CBF) for our publishing activities.

Printed in Canada.

First edition: 2014

Library and Archives Canada Cataloguing in Publication

Borden, Jack, author
    Faster, cheaper, better : starting a business in the trades / Jack Borden. — First edition.

(Business series)
Issued in print and electronic formats.

ISBN 978-1-77040-212-6 (pbk.).—ISBN 978-1-77040-956-9 (epub).—ISBN 978-1-77040-957-6 (kindle)

    1. Building trades—Handbooks, manuals, etc. 2. Repairing trades—Handbooks, manuals, etc. 3. Small business—Management. I. Title. II. Series: Self-Counsel business series

HD9715.A2B67 2014   338.4'7624068   C2014-905216-2
C2014-905217-0

Self-Counsel Press
(a division of)
International Self-Counsel Press Ltd.

Bellingham, WA   North Vancouver, BC
USA   Canada

Contents

Foreword   xv

Introduction   xvii

1 Faster, Cheaper, Better   1

   1. Faster   3

   2. Cheaper   3

   3. Better   3

   4. Good Project Management Will Help You Achieve
      Faster, Cheaper, Better   4

   5. Managing the Project Process   4

2 Considerations for Being a Self-Employed
   Entrepreneur   7

   1. Risks   8

   2. Are You a Self-Starter and a Hard Worker?   8

   3. Leadership   8

4. Your Specific Field of Expertise 9

5. Sell, Sell, Sell 9

6. Accounting and Financials 9

7. Responsible and Reliable 9

8. Life Changing Commitment 10

9. Money 10

10. Challenges and Heartaches 10

3 Business Fundamentals and the Business Plan 15

1. Required Skills: Sales, Production, and Accounting 17

2. Prepare a Business Plan 19

   2.1 Financial projections 20

   2.2 Write your business plan 26

3. Working Capital 30

4 How to Structure Your Business 33

1. Sole Proprietorships 33

   1.1 Incorporation with one shareholder 34

2. Partnership Options 34

   2.1 Unincorporated partnerships 36

   2.2 Partners in a corporation 36

   2.3 Partnership of corporations 36

   2.4 Partnership agreements 36

3. Should You Purchase an Existing Business? 38

4. Finding a Location for Your Business 40

5. Other Things to Consider 41

   5.1 Name your business 41

   5.2 Design a logo 41

   5.3 Insurance 42

   5.4 Set up a business bank account 42

   5.5 Reporting and registration requirements 42

   5.6 Business contact information 42

6. Legal 43

7. Human Resources 44

5	Prepare a Marketing Plan	45
	1. Purpose of Your Marketing Plan	46
	1.1 Define your market area and services	46
	1.2 Define your market size and your market share	47
	1.3 Find your target market	47
	1.4 Reach your target market	47
	1.5 Prepare your business message	48
	1.6 Marketing plan kick off	48
	2. Advertising	48
	2.1 Website	49
	3. First Contact with Potential Customers	49
6	I'm in Business!	51
7	Sales	57
	1. How to Be a Successful Salesperson	57
	2. Meeting Your Customers' Project Objectives	59
	2.1 Document the objectives	61
	2.2 Objectives defined and prepared by others	62
	3. Making the Bid on a Project	65
	3.1 Pricing the project	67
	3.2 Getting the price right	69
8	Produce It	73
	1. Project Management	74
	2. Create a Project File	76
	3. Purchasing Materials	77
	4. Contract Administration	79
	5. Construction Management	81
	6. Customer Relations	82
	7. Scheduling	83
	8. Managing Resources	85
	9. Mobilizing	86
	10. Supervising	87
	11. Quality Control	88

| | 12. Demobilization | 88 |
| | 13. Contract Wrap-up | 89 |

9 Account for It — 91

1.	Hire Someone to Help You	91
2.	Invoicing and Collections	93
3.	General Accounting	96
4.	Banking	97
5.	Job Costing	99
	5.1 Estimated cost to complete	100
	5.2 Projected over or under	101
6.	Asset Management	110
7.	Financial Reporting	112
8.	Cash Flow	113

10 Risks — 117

1.	Identify the Risks	118
2.	"Selling It" Risks	118
	2.1 Misunderstanding project objectives	118
	2.2 Customer misunderstandings about objectives and pricing	119
	2.3 Underestimating the cost of a project	119
	2.4 Bidding too low on a project	119
	2.5 Lack of understanding of a project's complexity and unforeseen conditions	119
	2.6 Lack of resources to undertake your project commitments	120
	2.7 Issues with subcontractors and suppliers	120
	2.8 Unscrupulous customers	120
	2.9 Poor relationship with the customer	120
	2.10 Lack of vision	121
3.	"Building It for Less Than You Sold It" Risks	121
	3.1 Not meeting your Customer's Project Objectives	121
	3.2 Project mismanagement	121

3.3	Not building the project Faster, Cheaper, Better	122
3.4	Not building it for less than you sold it	122
3.5	Inaccurate and unreliable cost-to-complete estimates	122
4.	"Accounting for It" Risks	122
4.1	Under capitalization	122
4.2	Not getting paid by your customer on schedule	123
4.3	The customer has financial difficulties	123
4.4	Personnel problems	123
4.5	Inaccurate and unreliable job-cost reporting	124

11 Suppliers

	Suppliers	125
1.	Supplier Credit	128

12 It's Time to Make Some Money!

	It's Time to Make Some Money!	131
1.	What Happens to the Profits in Your Company?	132
	Conclusion	135
	Download Kit	137

Samples

1	Statement of Earnings	23
2	Balance Sheet	25
3	Sources of Capital and the Implications of Each Source	31
4	Project Proposal	63
5	Project Types	66
6	Job Cost Estimate	71
7	Project Plan	78
8	Purchase Order	80
9	Paper Trail for Projects and Related Accounting Requirements	92
10	Invoice	95
11	Job Cost Report	102

12 Estimate Sheet   103
13 Work in Progress Report   108
14 Cash-Flow Statement with All Accounts Receivable
    Collected on Time   114
15 Cash-Flow Statement with Some Accounts Receivable
    Not Collected on Time   115

Worksheets

1   Are You Suited to Be a Self-Employed Entrepreneur?   12
2   Are You Ready to Make Personal Sacrifices?   13

Notice to Readers

Laws are constantly changing. Every effort is made to keep this publication as current as possible. However, the author, the publisher, and the vendor of this book make no representations or warranties regarding the outcome or the use to which the information in this book is put and are not assuming any liability for any claims, losses, or damages arising out of the use of this book. The reader should not rely on the author or the publisher of this book for any professional advice. Please be sure that you have the most recent edition.

Note: Prices, commissions, fees, and other costs mentioned in the text or shown in samples in this book probably do not reflect real costs where you live. Inflation and other factors, including geography, can cause the costs you might encounter to be much higher or even much lower than those we show. The dollar amounts shown are simply intended as representative examples.

Acknowledgments

Dedicated to my wife, Elaine, for putting up with and supporting a self-employed entrepreneur for more than 45 years.

I would like to acknowledge all the customers who entrusted us with their many projects during my 40 years in the construction business; without them there would be no book and there certainly would be no business. Also, I would like to acknowledge all of my 20-plus business partners over my many years in many businesses; all my accounting friends who have taught me a good working knowledge of their profession and who made me wise enough to know when to hire professionals. Special mention to Mike Stacey and John Barnes who both taught me a lot about project management. And I would like to acknowledge all of my competitors who have inspired me to be the best that I can be in my businesses; without competition there is no business.

Foreword

Workplace safety is not mentioned or discussed in this book. This is not meant to downplay workplace safety in any way. Everyone in our industry must know that workplace safety is of paramount importance to everyone working in construction and the related service industry. This book is about business and not necessarily the right venue to discuss safety in the workplace.

I encourage every reader and prospective entrepreneur to consider safety in the workplace and the safety of fellow workers at all times. As you read this book make sure that workplace safety is always on your mind and part of any plans that you may consider.

You should include workplace safety as an integral part of your business and be sure to create a workplace safety mission statement as part of your planning processes. A serious workplace injury or death in your business would be devastating. Don't let this happen to you or anyone associated with your business.

Whenever you see the words "Faster, Cheaper, Better," make sure you add the word "safer" at the beginning of this statement. You will appreciate the importance of "Safer, Faster, Cheaper, Better."

Always remember: Keep on the *safer* side of life!

Definitions Used in This Book

Construction industry: A business sector that provides construction services. In this book I have expanded the meaning to include related construction services such as maintenance, supplies, light manufacturing, etc.

Customer's Project Objectives: Customer is singular in this case and refers to one customer's defined objectives.

Customers' Project Objectives: Customer is plural in this case and refers to all of your customers' defined objectives.

Faster, Cheaper, Better: Your customers' primary project objectives.

Profit: The excess of the selling price of goods and services over their cost.

Project: An undertaking to achieve a defined set of goals or objectives within a defined beginning to end date.

Project management: The discipline of managing all aspects of, and all required resources for, a project in order to meet all of the defined project objectives.

Project Manager: The person responsible for all aspects of the project. No matter how small or large the project is, one person needs to be responsible for project management.

Project Objectives: Project objectives are all of the defined things that are to be undertaken and/or completed on a project. Objectives can include schedule, budget, and quality, and should be more specifically defined within a project scope of work.

Project Scope of Work: A document that outlines all of the details of a project, what is included, what is not included and, within the scope, defines all of the Customer's Project Objectives.

Self-employed entrepreneur: A person who works for himself or herself and who organizes and assumes the risks of a business.

Work in Progress (WIP): An accounting worksheet that calculates the value of work completed and gross profit earned on projects in progress at any point in time, typically at month end.

Introduction

This is a book about business; more specifically, it's about small businesses in the field of construction and construction-related services. Since this is a book about small business I decided to keep the book small as well. There are hundreds, if not thousands, of books written about business and most are a gazillion pages long and weigh in at a ton or so. This book is more to the point and focuses on better business practices for the hundreds of thousands of small businesses in the construction industry in North America.

Note that this book is all about starting and operating a small business and not the technical side of your business. I have to assume that you are technically competent and have good working technical knowledge and the skills that are required for your business. I also have to assume that for some trades in which licensing is required that you have completed all of the requirements for your state, province, and/or local jurisdiction. Therefore, from a technical perspective you are ready to go.

Throughout the book I refer to our industry as the "construction industry." Many businesses in the construction industry sector provide more than construction-specific services such as maintenance, supplies, light manufacturing, etc. No matter how your business is structured I'm sure you will benefit from reading and rereading this book.

You heard me right: there are hundreds of thousands of small businesses in the construction industry in North America. From excavators to framers, from cement finishers to roofers, from painters to plumbers; this book covers all of them. Our industry has built most of the infrastructure and buildings in North America and in the world for that matter. Sure, there are a lot of big businesses in our industry but don't kid yourself, small business is the backbone of the construction industry in North America. We are an extremely unique business sector when compared to other businesses throughout the economy. Big business, as we know, dominates industry and commerce and we are all familiar with big business names and entrepreneurs such as McDonald's, The Home Depot, Donald Trump, Bank of America, Walmart, Exxon, Apple, Royal Bank, Microsoft, GM, Warren Buffett; I could go and on. These corporations and individuals employ millions of people who are, for the most part, employees.

Where you will find the majority of self-employed entrepreneurs is in the construction industry. The average Joe or Jane couldn't even begin to imagine starting a business like Walmart, Microsoft, or Apple, but there are many people who have started or want to start a business in the construction industry. Why? The construction industry is very well suited for small business and for those who wish to be self-employed entrepreneurs. It can be relatively easy to start a small construction business and it can be fairly easy to get out of the business as well. Small businesses in the construction industry come and go; some last for a year, some for a decade, and some for an entire career.

Our industry is one of the more complex and unique industries in the world. Every project, whether it is a new development, a renovation, or a related service comes with a unique set of challenges. Our industry is not a production line making thousands and thousands of widgets or hamburgers that are exactly the same. Quite the opposite, because almost everything we do is customized. In order to undertake these projects we must have the necessary skills and resources to tackle these challenges in a sea of competition and demanding customers. Sounds like fun, doesn't it?

Our industry is also unique in that everything we do is made in North America. We may buy, resell, and install equipment made outside of North America but what we actually do in the field is made locally. We employ local people, we are part of our local business community, we support other businesses in our communities, and we are proud to say "made in the USA" or "made in Canada." Compared to the majority of retailers in North America who sell mostly goods imported from overseas, our industry can proudly say "made in North America."

The truth is, for many of us in the business, being self-employed entrepreneurs in the construction industry is the most rewarding career choice we could have made. Look at the alternatives. You could work for Walmart and rise to manager one day. Even if you participate in stock options you are still going to be an employee at the end of the day; one of millions. You could work for the government; whether it is federal, state, provincial, or local, and be set for life with a great pension after 30 years or more of service. You could become a professional such as a doctor, teacher, or lawyer. You could remain an employee in your chosen trade. With all of these choices why would anyone consider starting their own business in the construction industry and becoming a self-employed entrepreneur? Most likely for one or more of the following reasons:

- I want to be my own boss.

- I want to be in charge of my own destiny.

- I want the flexibility that comes with being self-employed.

- I believe I can make more money!

- I don't want to sweat my life away for someone else.

- I'll never have to look for a job again.

- I can take time off whenever I want.

For the most part these are very valid reasons; however, this is reality:

- If you are a self-employed entrepreneur you actually work for the toughest boss you could ever imagine; your own business. There is nothing more demanding than the demands of your own business. You will set the bar far higher for yourself than any employer would consider foisting onto an employee. In order to be successful, you will need to work extremely hard and smart for your business.

- Your destiny will be wherever your business takes you and that is very hard to predict. You will be able to choose but the successful pursuit of business opportunities will ultimately be your destiny.

- Being self-employed comes with a very flexible work schedule. Ask any successful entrepreneur and he or she will tell you that you only have to work half days; that is, only 12 hours a day.

- Making more money can be a reality but you will bust your butt and your brain for every dollar you make. There are no get-rich-quick schemes in this industry.

- As self-employed entrepreneurs, we don't have to sweat our lives away for a boss, we have to sweat our lives away for our business, our families, our customers, the bank, our suppliers, our employees and, at the end of the day, for ourselves.

- You may never have to look for a job as an employee again but you will be facing a lifetime of selling, and looking for new projects and business. It is a never-ending task.

- You can take time off whenever you want as long as there isn't a project in progress that demands your time just when you thought it was time for a holiday.

If you are still interested in this wild and crazy pursuit to become a self-employed entrepreneur, keep reading. If not, please pass this book on to someone you think may fit the bill. Who knows? If the person is successful, he or she may give you a job one day!

For those who wish to keep reading, all of the above points focus on what it would be like, and the commitment you need to make, if you want to become a successful, self-employed entrepreneur. In reality, you should be in business for only one reason, and that is to make money. That's right: to make money and lots of it! More money than you could ever imagine making working for someone else. The pursuit of profit in your business must be relentless and never ending. If this sounds like greed, it isn't. It is reality.

The truth of the matter is that without profit you don't have a business. Without profit you will become discouraged and want to quit. If there is no profit, your business can't expand and grow. You can't reward yourself for all the work and value you bring to your business without profit. If you're lacking a good income stream, you might as well work for someone else and avoid all the hassles and risks associated with owning your own business. Your bank will have no interest in dealing with you if your business doesn't make money. Without profit, your suppliers won't grant you any credit. You need profit; otherwise, you are going to have a very tough time meeting your personal and career goals. Without profit, your business will ultimately collapse. And without profit, you are a bane to yourself and to our industry.

There you have it. Why do you want to set up your own business and become a self-employed entrepreneur? To make money! Now you've got it. This is what this book is all about: helping small businesses in the construction industry and self-employed entrepreneurs make more money.

1
Faster, Cheaper, Better

Every customer has only three Project Objectives and they are Faster, Cheaper, Better. Contractors have been telling their customers for years that they do three kinds of jobs: quick jobs, cheap jobs, and good jobs, and you can have any *two* that you want:

- A quick, good job isn't going to be cheap.

- A quick, cheap job isn't going to be good.

- A cheap, good job isn't going to be fast.

What if your customer doesn't want to choose just two out of the three objectives? It seems logical that your customer wants all three: quick, good, and cheap. Or, said in another way: Faster, Cheaper, Better. As an extraordinary contractor, you can deliver Faster, Cheaper, Better jobs.

I am not saying Fastest, Cheapest, Best. I am saying that your services as a whole will be Faster, Cheaper, Better than your competitors. You may not always be the *Fastest*; you may not always be the *Cheapest*; you may not always be the *Best* in all aspects of the project. But taken as a whole on a project, you will be Faster, Cheaper, Better when compared to any of your competition.

This is what Faster, Cheaper, Better means:

- Faster: Always on schedule or ahead of schedule.
- Cheaper: Always competitive and providing the customer with good value.
- Better: Always a quality installation and a better project process.

Now here is something that is most interesting. Every Customer Project Objective that you identify and/or document will fall under one of the three categories of Faster, Cheaper, Better. What does this mean? There will be a number of documented Project Objectives, but in every case every one of these defined project objectives will fall under one of the primary objectives of Faster, Cheaper, Better.

If we were to take a sample project and have six contractors complete the exact same project, we know that one of the contractors will complete the project first, one contractor will complete the project for the least amount of money, and one contractor will have the best quality and project process. It's unlikely that one of the contractors will be number one in all three categories. But what if one of the contractors was rated as the contractor that was overall Faster, Cheaper, and Better when compared to the other five contractors? Isn't that the contractor that would be the real hands down winner?

The contractor who finished the project first may have incurred higher costs, so did his project quality and process suffer?

The contractor who finished the project at the lowest cost may have missed the scheduled completion date, so did her project quality and process suffer?

The contractor who had the best quality and project process may have missed the scheduled completion date, so did he incur higher costs?

Then there was the contractor who was rated overall as the best contractor when all three categories were taken into account. This contractor was overall Faster, Cheaper, Better when compared to all of the other contractors! That's the contractor the customer wants to do business with because he or she is likely the only contractor that met all of the project objectives of the customer.

Was this contractor the Fastest? No. But the project was completed on or ahead of schedule.

Was he or she the Cheapest? No. But the project was on or under budget and the customer was provided with very good value for every project dollar spent.

Was the contractor the Best in quality and project process? No. But the customer was provided with a job that met all of the customer's quality objectives and the project process was seamless and trouble-free for the customer.

As you can appreciate, this is an extremely important concept; it is the background for this entire book. Exactly what does Faster, Cheaper, Better mean and how do you achieve Faster, Cheaper, Better on every one of your projects? Let's define Faster, Cheaper, Better.

1. Faster

You complete all of your project responsibilities right on schedule. This means not a day late and not ahead of schedule if you are going to incur additional costs (earlier is okay if you are not going to incur additional costs). The customer said, "Be done on a certain day," and on that day you were 100 percent complete. Not 99 percent complete, but 100 percent complete. What else could the customer ask for? Cheaper and Better, of course!

2. Cheaper

You provide your customer with excellent value for every project dollar he or she spends with you. Yes, you expect to make a fair profit on the services you provide and the customer expects this too. What the customer wants to know is that every dollar spent with your company is going to provide excellent value. What else could the customer ask for? Better, of course.

3. Better

Better doesn't refer to just the quality of the installation. To the customer, a Better project means the overall project experience from beginning to end and the quality of the installation. A Better journey for the customer throughout the entire project! A project where the customer enjoys a trouble-free relationship with the contractor in which communication by the contractor is efficient, effective, and timely, and the contractor is committed to *meeting* the Customer's Project Objectives. The end result is a quality installation.

4. Good Project Management Will Help You Achieve Faster, Cheaper, Better

How is Faster, Cheaper, Better achieved? One way and one way only — excellent project management! Project management is the management of the project process from beginning to end. The project has been sold to the customer and you are ready to build it for less than you sold it. The project process starts and continues on until the project is 100 percent complete and full payment has been received from the customer.

Is project management mandatory? No. At the end of the day the light switch will still turn on the light on a poorly managed project just as it will on a well-managed project. The difference between a well-managed project and a poorly managed project is that on a well-managed project, Faster, Cheaper, Better will be achieved and a poorly managed project will likely be behind schedule, incur more costs, and the project process journey could be a disaster.

5. Managing the Project Process

A project is a task or group of tasks completed within a defined starting time or date and a defined end time or date. The project process is what takes place between the project start date and the project completion date. You complete a number of projects everyday throughout your life. For example, today I am going to the grocery store so I will get in my car, drive to the store, shop, return home, and put the groceries away. The project started when I decided to go to the grocery store and the project ended when I put the groceries away. Was there a management component to this project?

An unmanaged trip to the grocery store does not involve a pre-plan; it only involves the actual return trip and shopping. A managed trip to the grocery store likely involves the following process:

1. Make a list.

2. Check with your spouse or partner to see if he or she would like to add anything to the list.

3. Plan your trip to coincide with other projects that you may have to complete at the same time.

4. Plan your trip at a time that is convenient for you and when the store is not busy.

5. Stay on track and stick to the list by checking off the items as you put them in your basket.

6. Organize the groceries at the checkout in the best order for putting them away at home.

7. Return home.

8. Put the groceries away.

Here's the difference between a managed trip to the grocery store and an unmanaged trip to the grocery store:

- The managed trip likely took less time, therefore it was Faster.

- The managed trip had a list and you stuck to it, so your shopping trip was Cheaper.

- The managed trip avoided the rush hour and you didn't forget anything, so the entire process was Better.

Therefore, a project as simple as going to the grocery store, if properly managed, will result in a Faster, Cheaper, Better shopping experience.

Now I am not suggesting that you want to apply Faster, Cheaper, Better to every aspect of your life. You may end up driving your spouse or partner crazy. What I am saying is that in business every project process needs to be managed in order to produce Faster, Cheaper, Better results. Your customer is paying the bill so he or she wants Faster, Cheaper, Better, which means project management shouldn't be optional in your business. You need to manage every project you undertake.

Before determining how to best manage projects in your business, let's look at the fundamental field components of every project. Whether you are doing the field work yourself or you hire field personnel, you need to provide the following on-site for each and every project if you hope to achieve Faster, Cheaper, Better results:

- You need the material for the project readily available on-site when it is required.

- You need the tools and equipment necessary for the project, all in good repair, and readily available on-site when they are required.

- You need the skilled labor on-site, capable of undertaking the project tasks when they are required.

- One person should be assigned to lead the project process on-site.

- You need to provide clear and concise information (e.g., plans, specifications, drawings, scope, Customer's Project Objectives) to the project personnel that clearly define the scope of the work. Information should be reduced to bite-sized pieces and not in overwhelming package sizes.

- Project personnel need to be provided with clear and concise direction as to what the project expectations are (e.g., schedule, budget, project quality).

That's really all you need to do for the site personnel to do their jobs efficiently and effectively. In my experience on well-managed projects, your typical poorer performers will perform at the level of your best performers. By managing all of the above processes you have just taken away any excuse your poorer workers could have to perform poorly. You have just made their jobs easy and no one on-site has any excuse but to work up to your performance expectations. Now, if you let the site down and mismanage any aspect of the on-site processes, your poor performers will typically crucify you, whereas, your good performers will try to work around your mismanagement and still get the job done.

The bottom line: If you fail to manage all the on-site required processes, you will not achieve Faster, Cheaper, Better and you won't meet your Customer's Project Objectives. On every project, at some point in time, you are going to have to provide the necessary project elements defined in this chapter, and throughout this book. Why not do it with good project management?

The following chapters will help you apply the principles of Faster, Cheaper, Better. The first question you need to answer is: Are you ready to be a self-employed entrepreneur?

2
Considerations for Being a Self-Employed Entrepreneur

Being a self-employed entrepreneur isn't for everyone. Take a look around at all the people you know and identify those who are actually self-employed entrepreneurs; you will find they are few and far between. Personally I don't consider professionals working as individuals such as many lawyers, doctors, and accountants to be self-employed entrepreneurs in small business. I consider the real self-employed entrepreneurs of the world to be Tom's Window Cleaning, Jenny's Electric, and Jim's Construction; these businesses are run by the owners and they hire one or more employees to help with the workload.

This chapter is not intended to scare you or discourage you from pursuing your desire to become a self-employed entrepreneur. The purpose is to give you better insight into what you are getting into and to ensure that you go into business with your eyes wide open. Where would the world be if it weren't for people like you willing to take the risk to become self-employed entrepreneurs?

Consider the topics in the following sections as you work through the two worksheets at the end of this chapter. The worksheets can be printed from the download kit included with this book.

1. Risks

What is the risk of becoming a self-employed entrepreneur? In life we take risks every day — when we cross the street, when we drive somewhere, or when we participate in activities. But what are business risks? At the top of the list is finances. When you say you are a risk-taker in business, it means you are prepared to risk your hard-earned money on a business venture. If the venture fails, you are going to lose money. Are you prepared to take this risk?

Other business risks relate to sales. What if you don't make enough sales to sustain your business? If you don't, you are going to go broke. Are you prepared to take this risk? Give this some very serious thought before you answer question 1 in Worksheet 1 at the end of this chapter.

2. Are You a Self-Starter and a Hard Worker?

Give some thought to the people you know. You probably know some hard workers and some slackers. You may know some people who motivate themselves and those who need a kick in the butt to get moving in the morning. There are also those people who have an extremely good work ethic while others are more focused on other aspects of their lives.

Now you need to assess yourself. You need to be very honest with your self-appraisal. Successful, self-employed entrepreneurs drive themselves; no one needs to prod them. Successful, self-employed entrepreneurs have an exemplary work ethic. Successful self-employed entrepreneurs don't work hard only physically; they work with a focus on every task they undertake and are driven to succeed. Who are you? Are you one of them?

3. Leadership

You've probably heard the saying, "Lead, follow, or get the hell out of the way." One out of five people is a potential leader; three out of five people will make good workers; and one out of five people you don't want to have working for you. So who are you? Are you the one out of five who naturally leads people? Are you a take-charge kind of person? Do people look up to you and respect you? Do you have good interpersonal skills with your colleagues, family, and friends?

4. Your Specific Field of Expertise

Consider whether or not you are an expert in your specific field. Are you good at what you do? Do you pay attention to details? Do you think you can perform your job faster, cheaper, and better than your competition?

5. Sell, Sell, Sell

You will need to be able to sell your service or product. Consider whether you are a natural when it comes to sales. Are you confident in your ability to close deals? Are you comfortable in competitive selling situations? Are you comfortable dealing with potential customers? You will need to be a good negotiator as well as have a passion about the products and services you are selling.

6. Accounting and Financials

Most tradespeople don't have formal training in the fields of accounting, finance, or bookkeeping. How do you handle your personal finances? Can you prepare and stick to budgets? Are you organized when it comes to filing information and tracking expenses? You may not be an expert in this field and you may plan on hiring someone to undertake accounting and bookkeeping — maybe your spouse or a partner — but are you prepared to learn the fundamentals of business accounting practices and job-costing procedures? This is critical if you really want to understand what is happening in your business.

7. Responsible and Reliable

Are you responsible and reliable? These personality traits are fundamental to your success in business. Your customers, employees, suppliers, colleagues, and business associates will expect a lot from you, and they want to deal with someone who is reliable and responsible, someone they can depend on. Are there any personal things going on in your life that make you irresponsible and unreliable?

8. Life Changing Commitment

Don't take the move from employee to self-employed entrepreneur lightly. Works hours of nine to five will be a thing of the past. Leaving your work behind you when you leave the office or shop will be impossible. You can't let your business control your life, but it will play a major role in your everyday life.

Is your family prepared for you to undertake this life changing commitment? Families of self-employed entrepreneurs inevitably get involved in the business, even if it is just in a supporting role, so they will still be affected by this life-changing commitment. Consider carefully the questions in Worksheet 2.

9. Money

Why do you want to become a self-employed entrepreneur? To make more money is the answer. If you are not prepared to set the bar extremely high for yourself and strive to earn significantly more money than you would as an employee, then you may not be cut out for the regimen of self-employment. This isn't about greed; this is about you and your company being very profitable and the profits from your labors providing you with an enhanced lifestyle. That's how it works for successful, self-employed entrepreneurs.

10. Challenges and Heartaches

Unfortunately, challenges and heartaches come with the territory when you are a self-employed entrepreneur. Things that may happen in your business will have a greater impact on you than on your employees. Remember, employees can walk away, although they may walk away without a job. You can't walk away — at least not without doing significant damage to your reputation and financial security.

Before you begin a career as a self-employed entrepreneur, you should answer the following questions honestly. Answer and grade the questions in Worksheet 1 to get an idea of where you stand. This is not a scientifically proven test but can act as a good indicator of whether or not you are suited to be a self-employed entrepreneur. (You can print a copy of this worksheet by going to the download kit included with this book.)

Keep in mind that a low score in this analysis identifies an individual as an excellent employee as well; an excellent employee who has the option to become a self-employed entrepreneur.

If you answer "no" to any of the questions in Worksheet 2, then regardless of your score you should abandon any thoughts of becoming a self-employed entrepreneur. Again, this is not intended to scare away potential self-employed entrepreneurs but to ensure that you are making the right decision for you and your family. For successful, self-employed entrepreneurs, there will be some very good times, but along with the good times there will inevitably be some challenging times. It is these challenging times that make business people stronger and better at what they do, as long as they are prepared to make the commitment to succeed, no matter what the challenges may be, and to learn from their mistakes.

If you can pass the tests, and you still think that being a self-employed entrepreneur may be right for you, keep reading.

Worksheet 1
Are You Suited to Be a Self-Employed Entrepreneur?

Circle the number that fits your personality:

1: *I agree; this defines me and my situation.*
3: *Neutral.*
5: *This is definitely not me.*

1.	I am a risk taker.	1	2	3	4	5
2.	I am self-motivated and a hard worker; I don't need anyone to lead me.	1	2	3	4	5
3.	I am a leader and motivator to others.	1	2	3	4	5
4.	I am extremely adept at my specific field of expertise.	1	2	3	4	5
5.	I can sell myself, my expertise, my products, and/or my services.	1	2	3	4	5
6.	I am an excellent accountant, financial and cost analyst, and office organizer.	1	2	3	4	5
7.	I am extremely responsible and reliable in all aspects of my life.	1	2	3	4	5
8.	I am prepared to undertake a life changing commitment to become a self-employed entrepreneur.	1	2	3	4	5
9.	I am motivated by money and I want to make a lot of it.	1	2	3	4	5
10.	I am prepared for the challenges and heartaches that self-employed entrepreneurs inevitably encounter.	1	2	3	4	5

Score Analysis

10 to 20: You could make an excellent self-employed entrepreneur.

21 to 30: You may want to reconsider becoming a self-employed entrepreneur.

31 to 50: Spruce up your résumé and apply for jobs to become an employee.

Worksheet 2
Are You Ready to Make Personal Sacrifices?

Answer yes or no to the following questions:

1. Does my spouse, partner, and/or family support my decision to become a self-employed entrepreneur?

2. Do I want to sacrifice a significant part of my life, my free time, and my personal freedom for the sake of my business?

3. Am I prepared to undertake a life of worrying and fretting about my business knowing that there will be bad times along with the good times?

4. Will I be able to handle the stress that comes with money issues and will I be able to cope with the monetary risks?

5. Am I prepared to put my personal life and stability at risk?

3
Business Fundamentals and the Business Plan

Assuming you survived the reality tests in Chapter 2, and you are still determined to become a self-employed entrepreneur, this chapter will introduce you to some business fundamentals and how to write a business plan.

There are only three things you need to do:

1. You have to sell it (i.e., sell enough to sustain your business and make money).

2. You have to produce it for less than you sold it.

3. You have to account for it (e.g., all related requirements of financing, billing, payables, payroll).

That's it! There is nothing more to almost any business than these three things. It doesn't matter whether you are General Motors (GM) or Fred's Electric with only a few employees. The same three principles apply.

Take GM, for example: When its business got into trouble, what essentially happened? First, its market share dropped; second, its costs of production were too high leaving the company little or no margin on the units it did sell; and third, it essentially ran out of cash, which is a fairly significant problem for a company that is losing money.

When GM restructured, what did it do? GM focused on these three basic business fundamentals. It restructured its dealer network to give dealerships the best opportunity to compete and sell in a very competitive marketplace. At the same time, GM restructured its production facilities, renegotiated union contracts, and worked with its suppliers to significantly reduce production costs. GM also, as all of us taxpayers know, was able to restructure the financing for its business in order to have the cash needed to move forward.

When we look at the new GM today, it is selling a lot more units. GM's costs are in line, so the company is making money, and it has arranged appropriate financing for its business. Essentially all GM has done is: The company is selling its product; it is producing what it sells for less than it once sold them; and it is accounting for it. Voila! GM is back on solid business ground. It is essentially that simple when it comes to the three business fundamentals, but each fundamental can be complex in its own right.

You may think it a little strange to be comparing Fred's Electric to GM, but when it comes to business (and that means every business, large or small), they all have to meet the same three objectives. If they don't, they will fail. It's as simple as that!

I have one more theory when it comes to determining which self-employed entrepreneurs will be most successful. Since there are only three things in business that you need to do, you should be extremely adept at two out of three and have a good working knowledge of the third. For example, if you are a very good salesperson and you are extremely adept at something technical or production, then you should at least have a good working knowledge of the accounting end of the business. Or, you could be very adept at production and accounting but sales aren't your forte. Or maybe you are a super salesperson and great at accounting and finance but you are not strong at the production end of the business. No matter which category you fall into, you must take the necessary steps to acquire that "good working knowledge" of the area where you may be weak and ensure you continue to hone your skills in the other two areas so you remain extremely adept. All three business functions must be working like a well-oiled machine in your business or you will never achieve the primary objectives of *Faster, Cheaper, Better*.

The following sections discuss these business fundamentals in more detail.

1. Required Skills: Sales, Production, and Accounting

First of all, let's consider the most common scenario: You can sell it and you can produce it for less than you sold it, but your weakness is accounting for it. Accounting for it is the easiest part of the business to hire or contract out. You may already know someone skilled in this area.

Or:

You can sell it and you can account for it but your weakness is production. Then you need to have someone in your business, a very capable foreperson for example, who can handle production for you.

Or:

You can produce it for less than it was sold and you can account for it, but you are not so hot at selling. Then you need to have someone in your business who can sell. This can be a very difficult role to fill, but absolutely necessary if your business is to succeed.

Or:

You are extremely adept at all three basic business functions: You can sell it, you can produce it for less than you sold it, and you can account for it. If this is you, then why the heck are you reading this book? Just kidding! I am hopeful that you will benefit from this book no matter what role you may play in your business.

What are the skills, knowledge, aptitude, and attitude of the people who are successful at each function? Read on to find out.

I'll discuss sales in more detail in Chapter 7, but here's an overview of what you need to do when it comes to sales:

- Develop and retain meaningful long-term relationships with your customers that will result in ongoing exceptional sales results.

- Have the ability and determination to document your Customer's Project Objectives and to follow them up with a proposal that, when implemented, will meet your Customer's Project Objectives.

- Be committed to your customers' needs and expectations.

- Have exceptional knowledge of your products and services and be constantly updated to ensure you have the latest in information and product development from your suppliers.

- Be competitive. This does not always mean you have to be the cheapest but you should always price competitively.

- Communicate, communicate, communicate. Your customers need to know that you are available and an excellent communicator.

Most important, you are the person and/or company with which your customer wants to do business.

Chapter 8 will give you more information about production. For now this is what you need to know: You need to have the ability and determination to meet your Customer's Project Objectives as defined by the proposal presented to the customer at the selling stage — without fail.

You'll find more detailed information about accounting in Chapter 9, but for now these are the types of skills you'll need to know when you are starting your business:

- Exceptional general accounting and job-cost accounting skills.

- Commitment to providing timely, accurate, and reliable accounting reports and information.

- Timely issuance of accurate and reliable invoices to customers that provide customers with the information they require as defined in the Customers' Project Objectives proposal document.

- Relentless pursuit of accounts receivable that you require to be paid on time in accordance with agreed-on terms and conditions.

- Ability to manage day-to-day accounting and administration requirements.

- Exceptional information management skills.

- Communication: You are an exceptional communicator both internally and externally to the business.

Who are these people that do all of the above supermen and superwomen? No, they are ordinary businesspeople with a commitment to being exceptional at what they do. Almost everyone can be exceptional if they try.

Now that you have a better understanding of the business fundamentals, you need to create your business plan taking all of the above into account.

2. Prepare a Business Plan

Your business plan is going to be the roadmap for your business. A detailed business plan along with financial projections is going to give you insight into whether this is going to be a viable operation or not. Your business plan is going to set realistic goals, objectives, and projections and will define how you are going to meet these goals and objectives.

At this stage your business plan may be fictional, but keep in mind when you put your business plan into action you will be held to account for every last word and commitment you have made. You must be realistic and honest with yourself. No one has ever implemented a business plan that showed that the business had no chance of succeeding; if they did, they must have had money and time to burn. However, many business plans are created by "wishful thinking" and project some great results, but they are not reality. Proceeding into business with a flawed business plan would be your first step towards failure and possible financial ruin. This book is all about how to succeed, not how to fail, and the very first step is a business plan that is realistic, implementable, and clearly demonstrates how your business is going to succeed and continue to be successful.

2.1 Financial projections

I prefer to start my business plans with *pro forma* financial projections that are made up of two integrated financial documents: a balance sheet and a statement of earnings (income statement). In some cases readers of your business plan will also want cashflow projections, which I will discuss in greater detail in Chapter 9. Of course the easiest way to create the *pro forma* financial projections is to build an MS Excel spreadsheet. (The download kit that comes with this book includes some samples of very basic financial statements that will assist you with the preparation of this part of your business plan.)

Have you ever taken a business accounting course and been asked to create a fictional financial statement? They are so much fun and you can make as much fictional money as you want. Believe me, the real world is a lot different.

For those of you who are adept at or have a good working knowledge of basic bookkeeping and accounting, you can skip this section of the book. For those of you who are new to bookkeeping and accounting, the following is a fundamental guideline. Remember, if you proceed with your business plan, you must acquire good working knowledge of accounting and bookkeeping. Being able to read and understand the financial status of your business is critical if you expect to be successful in your business.

2.1a Balance sheet

The balance sheet is a snapshot of the financial state of your business at a specific date in time. It lists your assets, liabilities, and shareholders' equity. A balance sheet is exactly what the name implies: Assets = Liabilities + Shareholders' equity. They are balanced.

Examples of assets are cash in the bank, accounts receivable, inventory, equipment, land, and buildings. Assets are broken down into *current assets*, which are assets that can readily be converted into cash; and *noncurrent assets* that are fixed or long-term.

Examples of liabilities are lines of credit, accounts payable, and bank loans. Liabilities are broken down into *current liabilities*, which are liabilities that are due to be paid within one year or less; and *noncurrent liabilities* that are repaid over a longer term. Shareholders' loans to the company to provide the company with working capital can be listed under noncurrent liabilities.

Shareholders' equity is the value of your investment in your business. It is made up of capital stock for companies and retained earnings.

2.1b Statement of earnings and retained earnings

The statement of earnings is a record of financial transactions that have taken place in your business over a defined period of time. The statement of earnings lists your sales, cost of sales, expenses, and the resultant income. Retained earnings are also tracked from year to year.

- Revenue or sales: Revenue derived from selling goods and services.

- Cost of sales: Costs related directly to sales which typically wouldn't be incurred if there aren't any sales (e.g., project materials and labor).

- Gross profit: The profit before taking expenses into account.

- Expenses: Overhead costs which are incurred even if there aren't any sales (e.g., rent, management salaries, accounting, and bookkeeping).

- Earnings before income taxes: Earnings are recorded prior to determining income taxes owing. You will have earnings if your revenue exceeds your cost of sales and your expenses. You will have earnings if you have produced what you sold for less than you sold it for.

- Income taxes: Unfortunately if you are making money, you must make an allowance for income taxes. I shouldn't say "unfortunately" because if you have to make a huge allowance for income taxes, that means you are making a lot of money. Again, the primary objective of this book is to help you make a lot of money and pay a lot of taxes. Actually the tax bill will be between you and your accountants to figure out; I just hope this is a problem you have in your business. You've heard the saying that you are guaranteed two things in life: death and taxes. For self-employed entrepreneurs, we are guaranteed three things in life: death, taxes, and competition!

- Retained earnings: Basically, earnings that are retained in your business that are not paid out to the owners.

Before you start entering your information into the worksheets included in the download kit, try this exercise first.

Assume you have been in business for one year and this is the status of your business. Based on this information, create a balance sheet and a statement of earnings. Remember, this is fiction, not reality. I am providing some large, round numbers. Try breaking them down into the various secondary categories on the worksheet. For example, break the sales down into contract sales, material sales, and labor sales. If you are having trouble understanding this, now would be the time to seek some accounting or bookkeeping advice and training. If you going to become a self-employed entrepreneur, you are going to need these skills.

Note: In Samples 1 and 2 the numbers are purely fictitious that round up mathematically but are not a reality for any business. Only when you put your own projections into the forms does this statement take on some degree of reality.

Now it's time to create some financial projections for your business. You may find this to be a grueling exercise, but it is far better to deal with it now in a semi-realistic sense than to find out a few months or a year or two after you start your business that your projections were fiction at best.

- Revenue or sales: How much do you expect to sell in your first year in business? You will need to provide details on the source of sales and how you are going to meet your sales targets in the actual business plan itself.

- Cost of sales: Obviously your cost of sales must be less than your sales. The percentage difference is going to be your margin on sales. What is standard for your industry? Is it 10 percent (not enough), 15 percent (a tight margin in most businesses), or more than 20 percent? You will need to back up your projections in your business plan.

- Gross profit: Equal to your percentage of margin times your sales. For example, if you have sales of $1,000,000 at a 20 percent margin, your gross profit will be $200,000.

- Expenses: Don't underestimate your expenses. Most importantly, determine how much your business is going to pay you and include this in expenses. For smaller businesses you may anticipate working out in the field or on the tools

Sample 1
Statement of Earnings

Company name: ABC Construction
5-Year Projection (beginning January 1)
December 31 year end

Revenue/Sales	Year 1	Year 2	Year 3	Year 4	Year 5
Contract Revenue	50,000	60,000	75,000	85,000	95,000
Services Revenue	45,000	55,000	60,000	60,000	60,000
Other	5,000	5,000	5,000	5,000	5,000
Total Revenue/Sales	**100,000**	**120,000**	**140,000**	**150,000**	**160,000**

Cost of Sales	Year 1	Year 2	Year 3	Year 4	Year 5
Labor	30,000	36,000	42,000	45,000	48,000
Material and Supplies	40,000	48,000	56,000	60,000	64,000
Other	10,000	12,000	14,000	15,000	16,000
Total Cost of Sales	**80,000**	**96,000**	**112,000**	**120,000**	**128,000**

Expenses	Year 1	Year 2	Year 3	Year 4	Year 5
Administration	100	100	150	150	150
Accounting and Legal	300	300	300	300	300
Advertising and Promotion	200	200	300	500	500
Automotive	1,200	1,800	1,800	1,900	1,900
Depreciation	400	400	400	500	500
Insurance	500	500	500	600	600
Interest and Bank Charges	200	200	200	200	200
Office Expenses	100	100	200	200	200
Property Taxes					
Rent	1,100	1,300	1,500	1,500	1,500
Repairs and Maintenance	100	100	100	100	100
Salaries	5,000	6,000	7,000	7,500	8,000
Supplies	50	150	150	150	150
Telephone	600	600	600	600	600
Training	50	150	200	200	200
Travel					
Utilities	100	100	100	100	100
Other			500	500	500
Other					500
Total Expenses	**10,000**	**12,000**	**14,000**	**15,000**	**16,000**

	Year 1	Year 2	Year 3	Year 4	Year 5
Earnings before Income Taxes	10,000	12,000	14,000	15,000	16,000
Income Taxes	2,500	3,000	3,500	3,750	4,000
Net Earnings	7,500	9,000	10,500	11,250	12,000

Retained Earnings Beginning of Year		7,500	14,000	21,500	29,250
Dividends Paid		2,500	3,000	3,500	7,500
Retained Earnings End of Year	7,500	14,000	21,500	29,250	33,750

(working in a production role on the site). In this case a portion of your wages may be included in cost of sales. What is a reasonable percentage for expenses in our industry? Typically around 10 percent, but this may vary from business to business and industry to industry. Earnings before income taxes: If your gross profit is 20 percent and your expenses are 10 percent, then your earnings before income taxes will be 10 percent. Think about this for a minute. For every dollar you make in sales you get to earn one thin dime. It doesn't sound like much does it? Think about how hard you are going to have to work for that one dime.

- Income taxes: After all that hard work, you have to pay taxes on all those dimes you have busted your butt to earn. An allowance for taxes will depend on your federal, state or provincial, and local tax laws. You will need to consult a professional to determine the allowance you should make for current and future taxes.

- Retained earnings: In this scenario, assuming you are going to retain the earnings in your business, you now have $100,000 in retained earnings, less whatever tax allowances you are going to make, which could be anywhere from 0 to 25 percent or more. Now create your balance sheet and try to figure out where that $100,000 is, because it's probably not in the bank.

- Assets: Your projections are for year one in your business, so you are going to have some assets. You are going to have some money in the bank, you are going to have accounts receivable, and you may have bought some fixed assets.

- Liabilities: You may owe suppliers and employees for costs related to your sales. Have you set up a line of credit at the bank? List shareholders' loans here as well.

Sample 2
Balance Sheet

Company name: ABC Construction
5-Year Projection (beginning January 1)
December 31 year end

Assets	Jan 1 Year 1	Dec 31 Year 1	Dec 31 Year 2	Dec 31 Year 3	Dec 31 Year 4	Dec 31 Year 5
Current Assets						
Cash	10,000	6,000	7,000	9,000	10,000	12,000
Accounts Receivable: Trades		10,000	12,000	14,000	15,000	16,000
Accounts Receivable: Holdbacks		5,000	6,000	7,000	8,000	10,000
Work in Progress		2,400	3,000	4,000	6,000	7,500
Inventory		2,000	2,500	2,500	2,500	2,500
Prepaid Expenses		100	500	500	500	500
Other			1,000	1,500	2,000	2,000
Other					1,500	1,500
Total Current Assets	**10,000**	**25,000**	**32,000**	**38,500**	**45,500**	**52,000**
Noncurrent Assets						
Equipment		2,000	5,000	9,000	13,000	18,000
Other						
Total Noncurrent Assets		**2,000**	**5,000**	**9,000**	**13,000**	**18,000**
Total Assets	**10,000**	**27,500**	**37,000**	**47,500**	**58,500**	**70,000**

Liabilities	Jan 1 Year 1	Dec 31 Year 1	Dec 31 Year 2	Dec 31 Year 3	Dec 31 Year 4	Dec 31 Year 5
Current Liabilities						
Bank Overdraft						
Accounts Payable		5,000	6,000	7,000	8,000	10,000
Wages and Benefits Payable		2,500	3,500	4,000	4,500	4,750
Income Taxes Payable		2,500	3,000	3,500	3,750	4,000
Other						
Total Current Liabilities		**10,000**	**12,500**	**14,500**	**16,250**	**18,750**
Noncurrent Liabilities						
Long-Term Debt						
Deferred Income Taxes						
Shareholders' Loan	9,000	9,000	7,000	5,000	3,000	
Other						
Total Noncurrent Liabilities	**9,000**	**9,000**	**7,000**	**5,000**	**3,000**	
Total Liabilities	**9,000**	**19,000**	**19,500**	**19,500**	**19,250**	**18,750**
Shareholders' Equity						
Capital Stock	1,000	1,000	1,000	1,000	1,000	1,000
Retained Earnings Beginning of Period			7,500	16,500	27,000	38,250
Net Earnings		7,500	9,000	10,500	11,250	12,000
Retained Earnings End of Period		7,500	16,500	27,000	38,250	50,250
Total Capital Stock and Retained Earnings	**1,000**	**8,500**	**17,500**	**28,000**	**39,250**	**51,250**
Total Liabilities and Shareholders' Equity	**10,000**	**27,500**	**37,000**	**47,500**	**58,500**	**70,000**

- Shareholders' equity: For the purposes of this exercise if you have earned $100,000 less tax allowances you will have this amount in retained earnings.

The beauty of the MS Excel spreadsheets is that now you can do a number of "what-ifs." Reduce your sales to $500,000 and double your salary and see what happens. Assume that you are not going to work on the tools and your entire salary is going to be overhead and see what happens. Keep doing what-ifs until your projections begin to become realistic.

2.2 Write your business plan

Now it's time to actually write your business plan.

The reason I like to do the *pro forma* projections before actually writing the plan is that the *pro forma* exercise immerses you into the business that you envision. Assuming you have done enough "what-ifs," you should now have created a projected set of financial statements that you honestly believe are achievable. Now prove it, or at least prove it to the best of your ability. Remember, first you have to convince yourself, then you have to convince others who may be lending you money or investing in your business. You want readers of your plan, including yourself, to experience an ever-increasing level of confidence in you and your business as the business plan is read and understood. As a reader of your plan, I want to come away with the feeling that this is a plan that will work, this is the foundation for a successful business, and with a very high level of confidence in the principals and principles of the business.

Your plan is obviously going to demonstrate how you understand the three fundamentals of business and how you are going to accomplish these fundamentals. You also need to clarify where your expertise lies. Which two fundamentals are you extremely adept at and which one do you have (or you are going to develop) a good working knowledge of? Your business plan will likely be about five pages long plus your financial projections. For more complex businesses the plan may be longer, and for simpler businesses it may be shorter.

The first step in writing your plan is to explain to the reader what your business is. This is critical. Keep in mind that others who may read your plan may not know anything about your industry or businesses like you the one are proposing. You want your explanation to be clear and concise and about a page long. For example, after I read the first page of your business plan, I should understand that this plan is for a real business and have a basic understanding of what the business is all about and what the business does.

The second step is to tell the reader about yourself: Who you are and what your experience is in the industry. Explain why you are suited to be a self-employed entrepreneur and why you want to be a self-employed entrepreneur. Demonstrate that, of the three business fundamentals, you are extremely adept at two out of three and have a good working knowledge of the third. Now convince the reader this is true because it is true.

You should focus on your uniqueness. It is unlikely that you are going to state in your business plan that there are another hundred contractors in your area just like you and you are going to be just like them. NO, NO, NO! You are unique. Your business will be unique when compared to your competitors. Your approach to your customers will be unique when compared to your competitors. Your customers are going to want to deal with you because of your unique approach to your business. In fact, what makes you unique is your focus is on Faster, Cheaper, Better and meeting your Customers' Project Objectives. Now I can guarantee that most contractors in our industry cannot honestly make this statement.

Next, outline your goals and objectives, which include your mission statement, business principles, and values. I said I wouldn't mention safety, but obviously safety needs to be a key part of your plan. Quote your own unblemished safety record.

You will also need to describe how the business is going to operate. This means describing where the business is going to be located, the key people in the business, what plans there are for employees, who they are, and what they will do.

This all sounds really good, but now the reader is going to want to know three more things:

- How are you going to sell it?

- How are you going to produce it for less than you sold it?

- How are you going to account for it?

Sales, sales, sales! A person cannot survive without food and water. A business cannot survive without enough sales to sustain the business. A business suffering from a lack of sales will die a slow agonizing death. The reader wants to know how you are going to get enough sales to not only sustain your business, but enough sales to allow your business to be profitable, to grow, and to be successful. You will need to answer the following questions:

- What market research have you done?

- Who are your potential customers?

- How much do these potential customers buy?

- What is your relationship with these customers?

- Why are these customers going to buy from you and not your competition?

- How are you going to sell to these customers?

- How you are going to attract new customers?

- What geographic area are you going to work in?

- Are you going to specialize in any particular segment of your industry or are you going to provide a broader range of services?

Your sales summary and analysis should support the sales projections you have outlined in your business plan. Make sure you read Chapter 9 before undertaking this section of your business plan.

Now, as for production: You have shown how you are going to make sales in your business, now you have to demonstrate how you are going to produce what you sold, for less than you sold it, at margins consistent with what you have shown in your financial projections. Chapter 8 discusses production in more detail and you should adapt the message to your own business plan. Production is where Faster, Cheaper, Better comes to the forefront. You have told your customer that you can produce the job Faster, Cheaper, and Better than your competitors and now you have to prove it, in writing, to the best of your ability.

Regarding accounting: Ideally you have now convinced the reader that you can sell, you can produce what you sold for less than you sold it, and you are going to demonstrate how you are going to account for it. Again, before proceeding with this section of the plan, read and reread Chapter 9. For most of us from the trades this is the most difficult section to get a good handle on. If this is the one business fundamental that you are not adept at, demonstrate how you are going to develop a good working knowledge of this fundamental.

Referring to your financial *pro forma* projections you need to outline the business's requirement for working capital and how this working capital is going to be provided. As a rule of thumb, working capital should be equal to 10 percent of your anticipated annual sales and you should have a bank line of credit equal to the same amount. If you reduce the amount of the bank line of credit then the amount of working capital should be increased by the same amount. For purposes of a plan with anticipated annual sales of $1,000,000, you should plan on providing between $100,000 and $200,000 in shareholders' loans to the company to use as working capital and to arrange a bank line of credit in the amount as outlined above. Do not, under any circumstances, create a plan for your business that does not provide adequate working capital. You will be doomed before you start and readers of the plan you may want to invest in your business and/or lend you money will be the first to point this out.

Your initial plan should be for five years. It can be a real challenge to create a long-range plan at this stage of your business development. Make sure your first-year projections are as close to reality as possible and then project realistic and achievable growth for subsequent years. If you proceed with going into business, it is very important to revisit your plan on a regular basis (at least once every six months) and to update your plan based on actual results versus projections. All of your projections will not be spot-on, so a plan update will bring the plan more closely in line with reality as the business moves forward.

There is an infinite amount of information on the Internet about business plans. Some of the information is useful and some is not. I would still suggest that you consult the Internet to do some basic research and then integrate what you have learned into your plan.

3. Working Capital

How are you going to finance your business? On day one you don't have any retained earnings so you have to rely on two things — working capital that you can put into the business and bank financing. How much capital do you need? This needs to be clearly defined in your business plan. If you are adept at the finance and administration side of the business, then your financial projections will determine the working capital required for your business. If you are not adept in this area, you should seek some professional advice to assist you.

More important, where is your working capital contribution going to come from? Ideally you will have saved enough money in order to start your business so you don't have to rely on other sources. This usually isn't reality for most start-up businesses. Consider the following sources of working capital carefully and determine how best to put your plan together.

Your business must be adequately capitalized. If your business is undercapitalized, even though you are making money, you could be forced out of business because you won't have enough money to pay your employees, suppliers, and other commitments. Consider the typical sources of capital and resultant implications in Sample 3.

Here are some more topics to consider:

- Is there an opportunity for you to have some sales the day you start your business? It's possible if through your contacts and putting in some extraordinary hours before your start-up day you secure a contract or two.

- Is this the right time to be starting your business? Timing is everything.

- Payment from your customers is always critical but during your first few months in business collecting payment from your customers on time may determine whether you can survive or not.

- Do you know your costs for every aspect of the job you may be bidding on? If you don't know your costs, you can't produce an accurate and reliable job-cost estimate. It's that simple.

Sample 3
Sources of Capital and the Implications of Each Source

Sources of Capital	What to Consider
Self-funded without taking on any personal debt.	• Excellent. Only your money is at risk. • Don't put your personal financial and living expense requirements at risk. You will still have to eat as well as pay the mortgage.
Funded by a personal loan from a financial institution secured by personal assets.	• Are you going to be able to service this debt out of your new business? • Your security is now at risk should your business fail.
Funded by a personal loan from a financial institution with a personal guarantee.	• You are on the hook now. If your business fails, you will have to repay this debt personally.
Loan from an alternate source other than a bank.	• You will usually pay higher interest rates and fees. • You will almost always have to provide a personal guarantee. • Will your business be able to make the payments on this loan commitment? • If you are unable to fulfill your commitments for repayment on this loan, what are the consequences?
Loan from a friend or family member.	• The absolute worst people to borrow money from are friends and family, but unfortunately this can be unavoidable for many new business entrepreneurs. • These loans should come with the same terms and conditions as if you were borrowing from a financial institution including security and personal guarantees. • Make sure all paperwork is complete, legal, signed, and witnessed before any money changes hands. • If you are unable to fulfill your commitments for repayment of this loan, the resulting consequences can affect relationships forever. Money owing gives people an extremely long memory.
Line of credit from a financial institution to support business operations.	• A line of credit would typically only be available if you have provided some working capital from another source. • A line of credit will be secured by company assets (e.g., accounts receivable, inventory, work in progress, and other assets). • Personal guarantee may be required. • Usually the amount of loan available will be determined by margining the current value of the security.
Loan from an agency to assist new businesses.	• This can be an excellent source of funding but be prepared to provide all the required information to the loan officer.
Government sources for new businesses.	• Check with your local, state or provincial, or federal offices to determine if your new business may be eligible for grants, loans, incentives, tax credits, etc. • Funds from these sources may be tied to creating jobs. • Be prepared to jump through lots of hoops.

- Are there any extraordinary risks that you may be taking on with a specific project? For example:
  - Unacceptable payment terms.
  - The customer and/or general contractor is not financially sound.
  - You are unfamiliar with some aspects of the project scope.
  - Overall project management is sketchy, inexperienced, or nonexistent.
  - Your bid is too low.
  - The scope of the work is poorly defined.
  - The drawings and specifications are unclear.
  - You don't have all the necessary resources in place to undertake the project.
  - You have not taken into account extraordinary project conditions (e.g., weather, site conditions, travel time).

The next step is to figure out how to structure your business, which is explained in Chapter 4.

4
How to Structure Your Business

Thinking about how your business will be structured should be the next step after creating your first business plan. As you move forward and your plan shows that your business should be viable you can incorporate much of the following into your business plan. I have kept this as a separate chapter though, because first and foremost you want to ensure your business plan is viable before you get to the next step of how to structure your business. There is no use spending time on business structure if your business plan isn't viable in the first place.

Assuming you are going to be the sole owner of the business and there won't be any other principals involved, you basically have two choices: You can be a sole proprietor or you can incorporate.

1. Sole Proprietorships

Setting up a sole proprietorship means you will be the only business owner. This type of structure involves the least amount of money, time, and paperwork to set up. If you don't have a lot of money for start-up, you may find this the easiest way to begin the business. As your business grows, you may eventually decide to incorporate. It is always a good idea to contact a lawyer and an accountant to discuss changing a business structure.

The benefits of having a sole proprietorship are that you are your own boss, you don't have to consult with a partner or board of directors, and all the profits go to you. The downside is that you will be liable for all the debts that the business incurs. For taxes, you will be required to claim all of your profits or losses on your personal tax return. Biggest disadvantage? Unlimited liability, meaning you will assume all the risks and debts of your business.

1.1 Incorporation with one shareholder

Even though you may be a single person entity you can still incorporate your business. There are advantages to having a corporation including limiting your liability and in many jurisdictions preferential tax treatment for small businesses. Be aware that in many cases, even though you are a corporation, your creditors are going to ask for personal guarantees for any debts you may incur. If your only purpose for incorporating is to avoid liability, this may not be possible for a new business. For established businesses you will want to avoid personal guarantees whenever you can.

2. Partnership Options

For many people the first question is: To partner or not to partner? Throughout this book I will mention my Complexity Index, which I believe is most applicable when it comes to business partnerships.

In order to determine the complexity of almost anything involving more than one person you square the number of people involved. For example, a sole proprietorship with only one owner will have a complexity index of one: 1 squared = 1. A partnership of two will have a complexity index of four: 2 squared = 4. A partnership of 3 will have a complexity index of nine: 3 squared = 9. You can go on and on and on. The gist is that the more people you have involved in your business the more complex the operation and management will be. You may doubt that a partnership of two is four times as complex as a sole proprietorship but it is reality. The moral of this story is that before you ever consider entering into a partnership, give serious consideration to the Complexity Index and ask yourself if it is something that you should do.

I have been involved in many partnerships throughout my career ranging from partnerships of two to seven partners; therefore, a Complexity Index ranging from 4 to 49. I have had my time as a sole proprietor as well with a complexity index of 1. The bottom line for me is that partnerships can be good but they have to provide benefits that far outweigh the increase in complexity that is introduced into your business.

Partners must complement each other's skills. What are the benefits of two plumbers going into business who both have exactly the same skills? However, there could be some real advantages to this partnership structure if all the partners complement each other's skills.

Some partnership pitfalls to be aware of are as follows:

- Failed business partnerships have destroyed more friendships and family relations than any other cause. (I don't have any statistics to back this up, except for my many years of business experience.)

- People change. The person you are contemplating going into business with today won't be the same person in five years.

- There is a chance your partner could get divorced during the course of your business partnership. This may be devastating for your partner and your partnership in a number of ways; for example, personal trauma that affects your partner's ability to do his or her job, the need to make financial settlements, and time away from the business to deal with marital matters.

- Don't choose a partner who has or who may be inclined to have problems with drugs or alcohol. Addictions like these can destroy a business or cause severe ongoing damage to the business's success.

- You could spend more waking hours with your business partner than your spouse; therefore, choose your business partner carefully.

If you are considering a partnership and you believe this is the best way to structure your business, then you have some choices.

2.1 Unincorporated partnerships

As partners you can form a partnership by creating a partnership agreement, so it would be similar to a sole proprietorship except there would be two or more parties involved. You would have all the same advantages and disadvantages of a sole proprietorship except for the further complexity added to your business.

2.2 Partners in a corporation

Corporations can be set up with more than one partner owning shares in the corporation. Share ownership does not have to be equal and different classes of shares can be issued to different partners for specific legal, tax, and accounting purposes. Again, there are similar advantages and disadvantages to a corporation owned by one individual.

2.3 Partnership of corporations

Another option is a partnership of corporations where each individual involved in the business owns a corporation and then these corporations form a partnership. There can be advantages to this structure but it does introduce a higher degree of complexity.

2.4 Partnership agreements

The backbone of a partnership is the partnership agreement. The partnership agreement is the key to how your business will operate with two or more partners. You can see already that just by bringing in one partner you have created a whole new complexity for your business. Sole proprietorships don't need a partnership agreement.

All partnership agreements should address the following key points:

- Specify who the partners are and what their specific roles and responsibilities will be in the business. In some cases partners may be silent, which means they don't have day-to-day responsibilities in the partnership and their roles and responsibilities will be restricted and more specifically defined.

- Clearly divide the partnership. Are all partners going to be equal or will there be disproportionate ownership for the various partners?

- Define salaries and benefits for all partners.

- Define bonus provisions for all partners.

- Define sharing of profits from the business.

- Define the requirements for working capital and which partners will be funding working capital to what degree, and whether or not there will there be interest paid on working capital accounts.

- Delegate authority and define responsibilities. Will one partner be designated as managing partner with defined responsibilities and delegated authority or will all responsibilities and authority reside with all partners?

- Detail management such as partnership business meeting frequency and a requirement to keep minutes and record decisions.

- Describe dissolution of the partnership, partners leaving and/or retiring, the buying out of departing partners, and responsibilities of departing partners.

- Describe what should happen if one or more partners have to leave the business for health or other related matters. (Consider a partnership of three where two partners win millions in the lottery and they leave the other partner in the lurch with the entire business. Stranger things have happened and a good partnership agreement needs to contemplate these potential scenarios.)

- Provide a clause for life insurance. Do the partners want to have life insurance to protect the partnership from the untimely death of a partner?

- Explain how business losses will be funded. What happens if one or more partners can't provide their proportionate share of the cash to cover the losses and the shortfall has to be made up by the other partners?

- Define the role, if any, spouses of partners will play in the business. For example, if a spouse will be involved in the business, what is his or her role and how will he or she be compensated? (If you really want to add complexity to your partnership, involve one or more of the spouses in the business. I am not saying it can't work, but it definitely increases the Complexity Index by many fold.)

- Explain what will happen if the business hires children or relatives of partners. For example, how will they be managed or dismissed if they don't work out?

- Explain the responsibility for liabilities that the business may incur and how the responsibility may be shared. Remember, when a partnership is sued for whatever reason all partners will be named and the claimant will want to specifically go after the partner who has the better ability to pay. The partnership agreement must contemplate this.

- Plan for succession. If you build a successful business, what are your plans for the future of the business when one or more partners want to retire?

- Include a clause about mandatory retirement.

- Include a clause about dispute resolution.

Your partnership agreement may require additional detail depending on the specifics of your business and its structure. This is a basic list of points that need to be covered. Your business and/or legal advisor will be able to provide you with advice in this area. You and your partners should hire a lawyer to draft the partnership agreement. Again, I stress the Complexity Index; none of this is required in a sole ownership situation.

3. Should You Purchase an Existing Business?

Many people fall into business because an opportunity presents itself. For example, you could be working in an existing business where the owner wants to bring in a partner or wants to retire and there is an opportunity for you. Therefore, you are falling into an opportunity that you may have never considered when you first started to work for the company.

Or, you could consider purchasing an existing business and all of the good and bad things that may come with that purchase. There may be some advantages of purchasing an existing business:

- An existing customer base, whereas with a start-up company you will have to build your customers, which can take time.

- An established business with structure, tools, and equipment.

- The existing owner could agree to provide mentoring for a period of time.

- Trained employees.

- You can be in business instantly.

Disadvantages and risks could include the following:

- Cost to purchase the business and what you are getting for your money.

- Gamble of reputation, in that a business may have skeletons in the closet that haven't been disclosed and may affect your future sales.

- You believe you are getting all the good employees but maybe these employees have different ideas, including leaving and going into competition with you.

- Many existing business owners believe their inventory, tools, and equipment are extremely valuable when it's time to sell their business. The reality is that the majority of the inventory has no value and should be written off and the tools and equipment are, for the most part, worn out.

- Consider the value of the goodwill. If you are buying customer accounts that you can retain, then there may be some value. However, what is the value of the goodwill if just after you buy the business some of the key employees quit and take the customers you were relying on with them?

- Creditors. What is the relationship with the business's creditors and what is the payment history of the company?

When buying an existing business, you will still want to make a business plan and all the other related requirements I have discussed up to now. In addition to this, you need to go through a series of inquiries and investigations to ensure that you know what you are buying. At a minimum you should do the following:

- Request financial statements for the company for the previous three to five years. If these are not available this should be your first indication that something may not be right. You will usually have to sign a confidentiality agreement prior to being provided with this information.

- Require the seller to disclose to you any pending liabilities, lawsuits, or any other issues that could pose a liability to the company in the future.

- Talk to clients of the business and determine the company's reputation. Will the customers continue to do business with you in the future?

- Talk to suppliers and determine the company's reputation and its status with the suppliers.

- Talk to the company's financial institution to determine if there is an opportunity for you to continue doing business with it.

- Thoroughly research issues related to environmental and related matters, if you are buying any real estate or other property involved in the business.

When buying an existing business that is incorporated, you could buy the shares in the business and as a consequence you will then be buying all the assets and liabilities. This can be very risky if you don't fully understand the liabilities you may be buying. However, you could agree to buy the business operations and specified assets only, thus leaving the liabilities with the seller.

4. Finding a Location for Your Business

Where is your business going to be based? If you are going to run your business from your home, and your local zoning bylaws will permit this, then this is quite often a viable option for a very small business. For all others, you will need a shop and office.

As you have heard many times when it comes to real estate: location, location, location! Typically in our industry, location isn't that critical but there are still a number of things to consider:

- Proximity to your primary customer base.

- Proximity to your major suppliers.

- Safety and security of the proposed location.

- Proximity to your principal residence; the last thing you want is a long commute to your office or shop.

- Proximity to appropriate housing for your employees.

- Proximity to major transportation hubs including roads, major highways, and airports.

Your next decision is whether to own your location or to lease it. If you own your land and buildings when you retire, they can be assets that will provide ongoing benefits throughout retirement. Financing businesses in our industry can always be a challenge and owning your land and buildings can be great leverage to secure the best possible operational loan arrangements as your business grows.

If you lease, you will likely be making significant leasehold improvements that will be written off during the life of your tenure and they will stay with your landlord's building when you leave.

You will also need to consider planning for expansion if you believe your business is going to grow. Relocation of an active business to a new location can be very costly; therefore, choose your location wisely.

5. Other Things to Consider

There are many things to consider when starting your business. This section will cover some of the more important topics.

5.1 Name your business

The first thing many people see is your business name. Ideally your business name will be meaningful, easy to remember, and provide customers with something they can identify with. Choosing a name can be fun but challenging at the same time.

Do you want to use your personal name as your business name? If everything goes well with your business, this is not a big deal; however, if your business fails, your personal name could be dragged through the muck along with your business.

To be sure the name you are choosing isn't already being used by others you will need to have your name choices vetted by a lawyer or person qualified to do a business name search.

5.2 Design a logo

You are familiar with literally thousands of logos already with all the businesses you deal with and all the products you buy. Which logos do you like or dislike? Which logos do you think are effective and a reflection of the business? Which logos that you have seen are absolutely meaningless and confusing? Go through the list in your mind and that may get you started in the right direction.

There are professional firms that create logos for a fee, or you can explore possibly less expensive alternatives by consulting local artists.

5.3 Insurance

Every business needs insurance. You will need insurance for your assets, including real estate, and to protect you from liability claims. Select an insurance agent familiar with businesses like yours to be sure your insurance coverage is adequate and that the deductible rates are reasonable.

Loss of income insurance is another consideration in the case of devastating loss that could affect your company's ability to earn income. You will also want to consider life insurance for your personal situation and your business. A life insurance professional will be able to guide you in this area.

Do not over- or under-insure. Make sure you have the proper coverage you need to protect yourself and your business.

5.4 Set up a business bank account

You will need to choose a bank. The choice may become obvious if you are seeking business financing. If you don't need financing, you still want a bank that knows and understands small business and wants to deal with small businesses in your community. Remember, a bank is only as good as the person you will deal with as your account manager; therefore, choose wisely.

It is critical that you set up a separate account for your business. Don't mix personal accounts with business accounts under any circumstances. Banks that cater to small business can provide you with banking options that will be right for your business.

5.5 Reporting and registration requirements

Federal, provincial or state, and local authorities have different reporting and registration requirements. You will need to consult with all of these agencies to determine your registration requirements. The registrations may include licensing for your business and specific trade, payroll taxes, workers' compensation, mandatory pension plans, corporate income taxes, and corporate sales taxes that may be federal, and state or provincial.

5.6 Business contact information

Customer access to your business is extremely important. You will need a telephone number, an email address, possibly a fax number (yes, many people and agencies are still using faxes), and other social media considerations.

Should you use your home number for your business? This can be a cost saving but may bring your business too close to home. With today's smartphones you can do almost all you need to do from one device. A word of caution: a constantly ringing cell phone may be customers calling, which will be good. But if your phone rings too often with non-business-related matters you won't be getting any work done; you may be talking on your phone all day.

6. Legal

When you set up a business, one of the first things you may say to yourself is: "I need a lawyer to help me with this." This is true.

First and foremost, you must remember that all lawyers are not created equal. Don't go to the lawyer that helped you with the purchase of your home because you know him or her. You need to hire a corporate lawyer who understands business law and how to properly set up a business. Good corporate lawyers should be available in your community, so take the time and do the appropriate research to find the best corporate lawyer suited to your business. Choosing the wrong lawyer may be like choosing the wrong spouse; you may not know it until it's too late and it has cost you a lot of money!

Lawyers are no different than other businesspeople; they are providing a service for a fee. You should research your lawyer and ask for references to ensure that you engage the lawyer that is best for you and your business. Remember that lawyers are not cheap and whatever your lawyer charges you, you should double, because every hour you spend with your lawyer is an hour you have spent away from your business not making money.

Beyond your corporate lawyer there may be other specialized legal services that you need (e.g., labor law and difficult collections). Larger law firms will have lawyers who specialize in different areas. If your corporate lawyer does not have expertise in other areas, ask for a referral to a lawyer who does. For example, labor law can be extremely complex and not every lawyer can give you the best advice.

7. Human Resources

Even if you hire only one person you will have a human resources (HR) responsibility. The legal aspects such as labor laws I touched on in the previous section relate only to more complex HR issues that you may encounter.

Local, state or provincial, and federal labor laws bind your business to a full range of legal obligations to your employees. Rules, regulations, laws, and information for small businesses are readily available on government websites. Become familiar with all of this information and your obligations under the law. It is your responsibility to be knowledgeable in this area; ignorance is no excuse for not following your local employment law.

Don't underestimate the problems that a disgruntled or mistreated employee can cause. Do everything right from day one and your life and business will be the better for it:

- Be a good employer.

- Treat your employees with respect.

- Fulfill all of your commitments under the law.

Mistreatment of employees will not help make your business a success, which means you are not following the criteria of being a Faster, Cheaper, Better contractor.

Union, non-union, or open shop (open shop is usually a workplace not associated with any particular union or association or where membership in a labor organization is optional) are other options that you may face or have to consider in your business. There is no correct answer for all businesses and you are probably best suited to know what is right for your business.

Be aware that laws vary from jurisdiction to jurisdiction and ignorance of these laws could result in your business ending up in legal turmoil beyond your wildest belief. Be informed and ensure that you don't expose your business to unnecessary risks and the potential of becoming obligated to conditions that you are not prepared for. You can lose control over certain aspects of your business if you are not informed and don't manage the situation correctly. Seek professional advice when necessary.

5
Prepare a Marketing Plan

Marketing plans are part of the business development process. The most important part of business development is sales. It is the sale process that ultimately results in you accomplishing something for all of your marketing and advertising efforts. Sales are the life-blood of your business, and without sales and without meeting your business' sales targets your business will die a slow or quick agonizing death. In other words: Not something you are hoping for as a new self-employed entrepreneur. An effective marketing plan leading to sales for your business is key to your success. Give this area of your business the time and effort it deserves. (Please note that sales are covered in more detail in Chapter 7.)

Note that before you get the opportunity to sell something to a customer you must make contact with the customer, and this is accomplished by marketing and advertising. Consider how people are going to learn about your business. This is where a marketing plan comes into play. You may have touched on this in your over-all business plan but you actually need a separate marketing plan for your business. Your marketing plan should cover the topics that are discussed in this chapter.

1. Purpose of Your Marketing Plan

Your business plan is based on you achieving your sales budget; anything less is unacceptable. You are going to face a number of challenges in your business but typically none more challenging than meeting your sales targets. You need customers to call you or you need to make contact with potential customers in order to take it to the next level of selling. How you meet customers or how they contact your business is the entire reason why you should create a marketing plan.

Here are the objectives of your marketing plan:

- To identify business opportunities in your market area.

- To define marketing and advertising initiatives in order to pursue these business opportunities.

- To create awareness with potential customers of what your business does.

- To bring business opportunities to the business.

- To meet potential customers and to develop a business relationship with these customers.

- To ensure potential customers for your business call or contact your business when they are in need of your services.

- To ensure that customers remember your business and that your business is in the forefront of their minds when they are need of the services that you provide. Customers have short memories so they need to be reminded of your business from time to time.

- To identify the need for repeat business with established customers.

1.1 Define your market area and services

All businesses have a defined area where they can effectively and profitably provide services to their customers. You need to define what your market area is geographically. You also need to define the services you can provide to your customers. You can't be everything to everybody; you have to clearly define what you can do and where.

Business growth is quite often tied to an expanded market area and expanded services. If this is the case, you will create a modified marketing plan in order to pursue these growth opportunities.

On day one of your business you will want to be somewhat restrictive on market area and services to ensure you can meet your Customers' Project Objectives of Faster, Cheaper, Better. Do what you know, do it well, and do lots of it is a good motto. Your marketing plan needs to focus on this.

1.2 Define your market size and your market share

There is a defined size of the total market for your business in the area you will be focusing on. You need to know this number in general terms. If you are wiring houses and there are 500 home starts in your area, then every year to what percentage of these homes do you need to sell your services in order to meet your sales objectives? If you need to do 50 a year, you are going to need a 10 percent share of the overall market. This may be a reasonable share for a start-up business. Keep in mind that your competitors will be counting on their share of the market, too, and it will be up to you to win your share of the business.

1.3 Find your target market

Every business has a target market: A group of customers that you want to do business with, that you prefer to do business with, and that you believe will be the best customers for your business. Clearly understanding your target market is key to an effective marketing plan. Marketing and advertising is expensive and time consuming and if you focus your efforts and dollars towards your target market you will find that your plan will be much more effective in costs and results.

1.4 Reach your target market

You can advertise. You can pick up the phone and call your customers if you know to whom you need to speak. You can make cold calls when you don't know to whom you should speak. You can meet customers at tradeshows and other business events. You can have friends and colleagues refer customers to your business. You can use social media. You can befriend your repeat customers. You can use your business location to entice customers to drop into your business.

Knowing and understanding your target market will help you focus on what you need to do to reach your potential customers. Don't be afraid of rejection; it happens to everybody who tries their hand at marketing. Forget the rejection and move on to other customers who do want to do business with you.

1.5 Prepare your business message

In a few words or less, whether they be written words or spoken words, customers want to know who you are, what you do, and why they would want to do business with you. Clear and concise information is the best format. In our industry we are not selling widgets, we are selling technical services, so it's important that your message is meaningful to the potential customer.

1.6 Marketing plan kick off

Assuming you are proceeding with your business plan you need to kick off your marketing plan to coincide with the start-up of your business. You would really like to have some business on day one so you may consider doing some marketing and selling before your actual business start date. That way you could start day one with some real sales.

The option of an early start isn't open to everyone; this may depend on your previous commitments and agreements. Special advertising campaigns and start-up announcements are something you may want to consider.

2. Advertising

Advertising is typically something you buy that exposes your business to potential customers. Here are some examples:

- Business cards.

- Handouts or flyers.

- Newspapers.

- Classified advertisements.

- Special newspaper sections and inserts.

- Ads in trade magazines and magazines that target your potential customer base.

- Posters.

- Ad mail that can be addressed or sent out to specific areas unaddressed.

- Billboards.

- Radio ads.

- TV commercials.

- Internet ads.

- Social media.

- Yellow Pages.

- Ads in other information books distributed to homes in your community.

Be aware that you can spend an infinite amount of money on advertising. Someone once said, "half of the money I spend on advertising works; the only problem is I don't know which half." Truer words were never spoken. You may need an advertising budget for your business, but you must spend this money wisely and be prepared to monitor the effectiveness of your advertising campaign. It is always best to try one or two methods and then measure their effectiveness. Drop the ones that aren't working and try some others that you think may work.

2.1 Website

Your business, no matter how large or small, should have a website. Almost everyone today has access to the Internet via their computer or smartphone and the easiest and fastest way for new customers to find your business is to search the Web.

Setting up a website has never been easier. There are lots of programs available to allow you to create your own website, or you might find lots of businesses that provide website development services in your community. Be sure to research them carefully and to check references.

3. First Contact with Potential Customers

You never get a second chance to make a first impression with a new customer. You've spent time and money to get to the point of first contact with your potential customer, so now you want to take this opportunity to ensure that the customer's first impression of you and your business is a good one.

It takes many times more effort and investment to attract a new customer than it does to retain an existing customer; therefore, customer retention is key to your business success. In our industry the key to good customer relations is ensuring that your services are provided Faster, Cheaper, Better than your competitors and that all of your Customer's Project Objectives are met. If you accomplish this, your customer will have no reason to go anywhere else and will want to maintain a long-term relationship with your business and provide you with repeat business for many years to come. What else could you ask for?

6
I'm in Business!

You wake up in the morning on day one in your new business and the first thing you say to yourself is "I'm in business"! You've gone through a lot already and you haven't turned a wheel yet.

- You've done your soul searching to determine that you actually do want to be a self-employed entrepreneur.

- You've likely spent hundreds of hours in preparation, planning, meetings, thinking, brainstorming, talking, seeking advice, and wondering if you are making a mistake.

- You've arranged financing, set up bank accounts, met with your lawyer to set up everything legally, set up an office (in-home or out of the home), bought equipment, named your new business, created a logo, have a business telephone, possibly rented space, created and printed business cards and brochures, and created an advertising plan.

You are ready to start your day and the phone rings, you pick it up, and you answer "Hello ... I mean, good morning, Mike's Plumbing, Mike speaking." There you go, you are in business! Whoops!

It was only your spouse calling to see how things are going so far. Never mind, the next call may be from a customer.

What do you do now? There is no boss to tell you what to do. Employees are staring at you looking for direction. You know this is where the rubber hits the road, but you may be unsure about a lot of things, even though this is your business. Now all of these sayings come to mind:

- "I guess it's time to put up or shut up."

- "You'd better lead, follow, or get the hell out of the way."

- "I'm my own boss now, I only have to work half days (which is actually 12 hours a day)."

- Rule number one: The boss is always right. Rule number two: If the boss is ever wrong, see rule number one.

- It may be the first time in your life you can't answer a question by saying, "Hold on a sec, I'll have to check with my boss."

You actually do know what to do:

- I have committed in my business plan to X dollars in sales this year and this is the first day of my fiscal year. I am going to meet my sales projections today, this week, this month, next month, and every month of the year.

- I am going to produce everything I have sold for less than I sold it.

- My accounting systems will be impeccable. I will always be aware of where I am at in my business with a real focus on job costs, cash flow, accounting, and commitments to lenders and suppliers.

OK, you have survived the first week and you are getting the gist of what it's going to be like to be a self-employed entrepreneur. The business is starting to take on some normalcy and you know what to do. This is your plan for the next week even though you know all plans are subject to change:

- Monday: You secured two jobs last week so you are going to take the day to organize and plan these projects.

- Tuesday: You are going to set up job-costing procedures for the two projects.

- Wednesday: You are going to the project sites to meet the key personnel and to plan the schedule.

- Thursday: You are going to organize supplies, equipment, and materials.

- Friday: You make sure everything is set to start both projects next week.

Here is what actually happens:

Monday:

- Today I need eight hours to put together the plan for the two projects we booked.

- It's only 10:00 a.m. and I've already had two calls from potential customers who received the brochures I delivered to their offices last week. I am meeting them this afternoon, one at 2:00 p.m. and the other at 4:00 p.m.

- The bookkeeper is new so we need to get together for an hour this morning.

- I think I'll eat my lunch at my desk and carry on with my work. There is no time to go out.

- Time to go to meet with the new customers.

- What a great meeting. The customer wants a fully detailed proposal by Friday at 4:00 p.m. and I think he wants to give me the job.

- The customer I met with at 4:00 p.m. has some upcoming work and wanted to discuss our experience and ability to take on her projects. I will send her some more information about our company later this week and meet with her again next week.

- Back to the office to complete my two project plans so I can send them off to the customers.

- It's 5:00 p.m. already and I still have a long way to go. Time to phone home and let them know I won't be home until 6:00 p.m.

- "Hi honey, I'm home. Sorry I'm late. I was swamped today. Maybe we should plan for dinner with the family at 6:00 from now on rather than 5:00. Or I can go into work early."

Tuesday:

- I start early to be prepared for the meeting with the bookkeeper at 8:00 a.m.

- At noon the bookkeeper and I emerge from a long meeting but with a very good accounting plan in place for the two new projects. The meeting was interrupted by five phone calls that I had to take from suppliers for the new projects and one more customer. I arranged to meet the customer at 3:00 p.m. this afternoon.

- I need to spend time now to take off materials, confirm quantities, and check project costs.

- Whoops! I just spilled some of my lunch on the job-cost spreadsheet. Better print a clean copy.

- Time to meet the new customer at 3:00 p.m.

- Wow, I can't believe the reception I'm getting from my brochure. I think people were just waiting for me to set up my business. Thankfully this customer's project isn't scheduled for a couple of weeks so I can work on the project plan next week.

- Time to head back to the office to wrap up for the day.

- I have three phone calls to return that I couldn't take while I was with the customer.

- "Hi honey, I'm home. Yes, 6:00 for dinner works a lot better!"

Wednesday:

- Another early start. I have a meeting at project one at 8:00 a.m. and project two at 1:00 p.m. I think these two meetings are going to take all day.

- I was right. I made it back to the office by 5:00 p.m. I can wrap up for the day and be home in time for dinner.

Thursday:

- I have five phone calls to return from yesterday.

- I will be busy in the office all day doing project planning, ordering, and scheduling for project one and project two.

- I have put together a package of information for the new customer I met with on Monday at 4:00 p.m.

- I am working diligently on the scope of work and estimate that needs to be ready for the customer I met with on Monday at 2:00 p.m.

- I have to leave by 4:30 p.m. today because this is my kid's soccer day.

Friday:

- Early start today to get everything done.

- Completing project planning for next week. Everything is ready to go.

- Completed the information for the new customer and put it in an envelope. I will drop it off this afternoon.

- Finalizing estimate and scope of work for other customer. I'll work through lunch to get this done.

- Time to go and drop off information for the new customer. This takes longer than I thought because he wants to sit down and review what I put together. This is very encouraging.

- At 3:30 p.m. I drop off the scope of work and estimate for the customer for the bid that closes at 4:00 p.m. I believe I have put together a very good proposal. I sure want that project.

- Wow, I am bushed. I am going home early. Why not? It's almost 5:00 p.m.

Saturday:

- I stop by the office for two hours to clean my desk so I can make a fresh start on Monday morning.

- Wow! What a week!

Guess what? The next week and the week after that, and the week after that will likely be just as busy, exciting, and rewarding. Be prepared because this is what you can expect to happen in your business.

What do your customers think? They don't care how busy you are! They don't care about your other customers, that your supplier let you down, that your employee called in sick today, and that you had an equipment breakdown. They don't care about your problems! They only care about their job and that you fulfill all the commitments that you made to them the day they gave you the job. What do you need to do to ensure your customers are getting the service they expect and deserve?

- You need to be organized.

- You need to be responsible.

- You need to be a good communicator.

Our industry has a terrible reputation because of contractors who are disorganized, irresponsible, and poor communicators. The first thing that you can do to make yourself and your business unique when compared to your competition is to be organized, responsible, and communicate.

Customers may understand when you communicate a problem or a delay, but not showing up on schedule and not calling the customer is a sure way to lose that customer forever. With today's communication equipment you have no excuse to not communicate. A few hints:

- Write everything down or record everything in your scheduler. (Every smartphone has a scheduling program.)

- Trust nothing to memory.

- Don't make commitments that you can't keep.

- Communicate, communicate, communicate.

- Always show up five minutes early for appointments.

- Call if you are going to be more than five minutes late.

- Take responsibility for your commitments.

- Be reliable; be the contractor that your customers know they can trust.

- Strive to be the contractor who is consistently Faster, Cheaper, Better when compared to your competition.

7
Sales

In previous chapters I've mentioned the first fundamental of business: Sell it. Without sales you have nothing. You certainly don't have a business. You've been buying things all your life and you've met some good and bad salespeople. You've met salespeople you want to do business with over and over again and others you don't care if you ever see again. You've met salespeople you will never forget because of the great service you received, the competitive price, and the follow up; all of those things that make salespeople successful. You've also met salespeople you will never forget because of terrible service, they overcharged you, and they wouldn't return your phone calls; all those things that make salespeople a disaster. What kind of salesperson are you going to be?

1. How to Be a Successful Salesperson

Some things bear repeating, and in this book this is very true. The following is a description of a successful salesperson from Chapter 3:

- Develop and retain meaningful long-term relationships with your customers that will result in ongoing exceptional sales results.

- Have the ability and determination to document your Customers' Project Objectives and to follow up with a proposal that, when implemented, will meet your Customers' Project Objectives.

- Be committed to your customers' needs and expectations.

- Have exceptional knowledge of your products and services and be constantly updated to ensure you have the latest in information and product development from your suppliers.

- Be competitive. This does not always mean you have to be the cheapest but you should always price competitively.

- Communicate. Your customers need to know that you are available and you are an excellent communicator.

- You are the person/company with which your customer wants to do business.

How do you become this person? Commitment is a good start because words are only words unless they are backed up by commitment. When a business makes the statement, "at our business the customer is king," these are very nice words, but what do they mean? Sure I would like to be treated like a king whenever I am dealing with a salesperson. But it won't happen; he or she certainly won't meet my expectations, unless the salesperson is committed to meeting my expectations. Now, here is the tricky part: How can the salesperson meet my expectations if he or she doesn't know what my expectations are?

For example, if I am shopping for a pair of shoes, what does the salesperson need to know in order to get to know and understand my expectations and objectives? I know, at least I think I know, what my expectations are. But if the salesperson doesn't take the time or make the commitment to discuss this with me, how will he or she ever know what my expectations are? I may not know exactly what my objectives are and I may need help from the salesperson to identify exactly what they are. There are things I can guarantee:

1. If the salesperson makes the commitment to know and understand my expectations and objectives, and he or she helps me to communicate my expectations and objectives, then there is a good chance that my expectations and objectives will be met.

2. If the salesperson doesn't make the commitment to know and understand my expectations and objectives, and he or she doesn't do anything to help me explain my expectations and objectives, then there is a good chance that my expectations and objectives won't be met.

3. If all of my expectations and objectives are met, I am going to be a very happy customer that will likely return time and time again.

4. If my expectations and objectives are not met, or only partially met, then I won't be returning there any time soon.

5. If I am a happy customer, and all of my expectations and objectives are met, I am going to tell all my friends and colleagues that this is a great place to buy shoes and to make sure they ask for salesperson "Jane."

6. If I am an unhappy customer, or I had a bad experience at this shoe store, I am going to tell all my friends and colleagues not to go there and especially not to deal with salesperson "Joe."

7. The salesperson with true customer commitment will be happy in his or her job, will be very successful, and will likely make far more money than many of his or her colleagues.

8. The salesperson who is not committed to his or her customers will be unhappy in his or her job, and will not be successful, and will likely earn far less than any of his or her colleagues.

There you have it. The salesperson who has the skills, ability, and commitment to get to know his or her customer's expectations and objectives versus the salesperson who may have the skills and ability but he or she doesn't make the commitment to get to know his or her customer's expectations and objectives.

2. Meeting Your Customers' Project Objectives

In the construction and related service business industry I always use the term "Customer's Project Objectives" when referring to one of my customers, and "Customers' Project Objectives" when referring to all of my customers. The same principles apply to our industry as they apply to the shoe salesperson in the previous section.

The difference is in what the customers are buying, not necessarily in the processes in which they make their buying decisions. In our industry our focus needs to be on our Customers' Project Objectives and how we go about *meeting* our Customers' Project Objectives.

I can make the same eight guarantees as I did in section 1. when it comes to meeting Our Customers' Project Objectives. We know now what we need to do, so how do we go about it?

If you really want to be successful, all you need to do is meet your Customers' Project Objectives. Sounds simple, doesn't it? But what are your Customers' Project Objectives? If you don't know, how do you find out?

Think of all the things you buy, the purchasing decisions you need to make on a daily basis, and the interaction you may need with the sales personnel where you are making your purchases. Grocery stores typically don't have to do a lot of selling. They provide convenience because they likely have all your needs in stock at a convenient location, you can select all the products you want, and you may never need to interact with a member of the store's staff, especially if you use the self-checkout. In this case the store personnel have anticipated your objectives when you come to their store, so they have done everything they can do to meet your objectives without actually talking to you. Pretty simple business!

Buying furniture is a different buying experience altogether. That's why you almost always interact with a salesperson when buying furniture. Like the shoe salesperson, the furniture salesperson needs to talk with you, to communicate with you, in order to determine your objectives. The salesperson can't be expected to be a mind reader; the customer has to participate in the process in order to relay his or her objectives to the salesperson. The Complexity Index comes into play in this situation. A furniture salesperson selling to a single person is dealing with a complexity of one; if it's a couple, a complexity of four; and if a couple have brought along a mother or mother-in-law to help in the decision-making process, the complexity rises to nine.

In our industry we are selling something that can only be envisioned, specified, drawn, planned, or verbally communicated. You can't buy a plumbing job off the shelf for your new house. So what do you need to do in order to hone your sales abilities to ensure you succeed in getting to first base?

In our industry we can deal with an infinite number of types of projects and service requests. That's why on any given project there are a number of trades providing a very broad range of services but seldom do you see one trade providing more than one specified service.

Typically, if you are an electrical contractor, you're not dabbling in another trade like carpentry for example; if you're electrical, you're electrical and that's it. How many different trades does it take to put a project together? One if it's a re-plumbing job, or maybe ten or more on a larger project, and many more on a very large and complex project. If you are a typical contractor, you are only concerned with your trade and your ability to get that part of the project for your company.

When you look at my selling philosophies, does one size fit all for all contractors and service providers in our industry? Generally yes, but all contractors will have to modify these ideas somewhat to fit the specific their selling techniques and needs.

2.1 Document the objectives

You need to put a proposal in front of your customer that will meet your Customer's Project Objectives. You'll need to make some careful considerations when making a proposal. For example, making a proposal like the following example is going to leave you hanging out so far that you could end up making a lot of money or losing your shirt. You have no idea, nor does your customer, on what the final outcome may be:

Per our verbal discussion on your project my bid is $1,000,000 and everything is included.

In this example, it says "everything is included." What does "everything" include? This is where you need to document everything that is included, and everything that is not included. You'll need to go a step further by providing information and supporting documentation that will convince the customer that if he or she chooses you, his or her project objectives will be met; whereas, if the customer chooses one of your competitors, he or she may be taking a risk that all of his or her project objectives may not be met. No customer in our industry can ask for anything more than having his or her project objectives met.

When you have a verbal conversation with the customer, he or she has communicated *some* of his or her project objectives to you. If you had a really good two-way conversation with your customer with lots of questions and interaction, you are probably getting closer to understanding more of your Customer's Project Objectives. However, if you came into the conversation fully prepared with a documented list of questions that you should be asking the customer, you may be getting close to knowing and understanding all of your Customer's Project Objectives.

I can guarantee that you are going to have one very happy customer if you've done the following:

- A good job of defining and documenting your Customer's Project Objectives.

- Agreed with the customer that the documented project objectives fully define the project scope and related project conditions.

- Undertook the project and met all of the defined Customer's Project Objectives.

If you think back in your career to anytime you have had to deal with an unhappy customer, I can tell you it will all relate to one or more project objectives not being met. If there were 100 documented project objectives on a job and you met 98 of them, you could still have a very unhappy customer because you failed to meet two project objectives. The key is to meet *all* of your Customer's Project Objectives — all those that are documented — no less and no more. See Sample 4 for an example of a project proposal.

2.2 Objectives defined and prepared by others

What about the projects where the Customer's Project Objectives are defined by plans and specifications prepared by others? This is the case on most engineered and architecturally designed projects. What input can you have on better defining the Customer's Project Objectives? In many cases, none.

Your job here is to ensure you understand the project objectives defined by others and to provide a proposal that meets those defined objectives — not exceeds the defined objectives, *meets* the defined objectives. You are only going to get paid to meet the

Project Proposal

ABC Construction Company
Project Proposal

Project:
ABC Estimate No.:
Date:

Customer: Smith Building
Name:
Address:
Contact Information:

We are pleased to submit our quotation/proposal to undertake this work.

Scope of Work
Supply and install concrete, piping, lumber, and steel in accordance with issued plans and specifications.

Plans and Specifications
Plans and specifications were issued by the owner and the following information was provided to ABC Construction Company:

- Drawings 1, 2, and 3 dated March 1.
- Specification dated March 1.
- Addendum number 1 dated March 15.
- Site meeting minutes and clarifications dated March 8.

Not Included
The following items are not included in our project proposal:

- Painting.
- Roofing.
- Project delays that are not the responsibility of ABC Construction Company.
- Sales taxes (will be charged separately).

Schedule
Start date: April 15
Completion date: August 31

Customer's Project Objectives
During the course of our review of this project and based on information provided we have determined that the following objectives for this project must be met. ABC Construction Company is committed to meeting these objectives on your project:

- The project will be started and completed on schedule.
- ABC Construction Company will advise the customer of any proposed contract changes that may affect the overall project cost prior to any additional costs being incurred.
- ABC Construction Company will ensure that all construction meets the specifications as issued.

Project Safety
(See FCB foreword. Always provide the customer with your safety record and commitment to safety. This is important to everyone even if the customer hasn't asked for it.)

Contract Administration
ABC Construction Company will issue project invoices on the 20th of each month to accommodate the Smith Building accounting requirements.

Terms and Conditions
All issued invoices are to be paid in full by the 15th of the month. We cannot accept delay of payment under any circumstances.

Holdback
Holdbacks of any kind are not applicable to this project.

Quotation
ABC Construction Company's quotation for this scope of work and related terms and conditions is SEVENTY-FIVE THOUSAND DOLLARS ($75,000.00).

Approval to Proceed
If you accept this proposal, please sign below and return a copy of this proposal to our office.

We accept this proposal from ABC Construction Company.

_____

Customer Name and Authorization

_____

Date

defined project objectives; if you exceed them and you incur additional costs, those costs are going to come out of your pocket. The customer is paying you to meet the defined project objectives and nothing more.

3. Making the Bid on a Project

Is price all that really matters? Unfortunately, that is the case on many bid projects; the lowest bid gets the job unless there are extenuating circumstances.

The other unfortunate aspect of this process is that the customer will almost always believe that the lowest bidder is right and all of the other bidders are being greedy or not being competitive. But how else is the customer to know? For the customer the path of least resistance is to believe the lowest bidder. After all, there is one thing that every customer knows and that is that one is less than two — which means anyone can pick the lowest bidder.

If a customer ever decides not to pick the lowest bidder, what criteria will the person use to make this decision? If he or she is a smart customer, the person will determine that the low bidder in addition to having the lowest price must meet all of the project objectives. If there is any doubt that the low bidder won't meet all of the project objectives, the customer has to balance the benefit of low price against the odds of all project objectives not being met.

Your bid, combined with your reputation of always meeting your Customer's Project Objectives will almost always put your bid up for consideration. Of course, if you have the best proposal combined with the best price, you and the customer are going to do business together.

There are numerous kinds of projects that you may bid on in your business. Knowing and understanding how the customer is going to make his or her buying decision is important when it comes to determining how you should approach the project and how you put together your strategy to be successful. Sample 5 includes some of the various types of projects that you may encounter.

You can almost be guaranteed competition when you are pursuing a project. In fact, you should always assume you *will* have competition.

Project Types

Type of Project	Project Objectives Defined By	Project Award Criteria	What Can You Do to Influence the Buying Decision?
Fully designed and specified by others typically by engineers and/or architects.	Defined within the specification and documents prepared by others.	Cheaper (primarily) Faster (always a consideration) Better (always a consideration)	• Pre-bid qualification. • Preferred bidder status. • Customer relations pre-bid. • Provide pre-bid or with the bid-supporting documentation that convinces the customer that you are the best choice to ensure that the Customer's Project Objectives will all be met.
Design build.	You will define the specifications and documents.	Faster, Cheaper, Better	• Ensure the customer that you are the company that will meet all of the project objectives including Faster, Cheaper, Better. • Customer relationships. • Your reputation.
Customer specified requirements and objectives.	Although the customer may have defined the project objectives, you can enhance the list based on your experience.	Depending on the customer. Sophisticated customers will analyze the contractor based on Faster, Cheaper, Better. Unsophisticated customers will go by price alone.	• Ensure the customer that you are the company that will meet all of the project objectives including Faster, Cheaper, Better. • Customer relationships.

To pursue a project you should do everything you can to position yourself as the preferred bidder/contractor. Customers almost always have a preferred contractor when they ask for a bid and this should be you. How do you position yourself as the preferred contractor?

• Customer relationship prior to the bidding process.

• Pre-bid meetings, information, and/or presentations.

• Pre-bid identification and documentation of your Customer's Project Objectives.

• Demonstrating to your customer that you are the best choice to ensure that the Customer's Project Objectives will be met.

This is what you want the customer to be thinking as you go through the pre-bid sales process:

- This contractor is very interested in our project.

- This contractor is asking all the right questions.

- This contractor has a good understanding of what our project is all about and what our objectives are.

- This contractor is proving to us that his company is the best choice for us and should be our preferred contractor.

- I hope this contractor can combine all of these good things she is saying with a competitive proposal.

This all sounds good in theory, but what about those projects in which the customer's sole decision-making criteria is price and nothing else? This is certainly the case on many projects. However, in some cases, you will wake up the customer to the fact that there should be more to his or her decision-making criteria than price, and when taking into account the overall project objectives, price should be only one factor of many to be considered.

Now that the pre-bid process is complete and the time has come for you to put together your proposal along with a price, where do you go from here? Begin by updating the documentation of your Customer's Project Objectives and then make sure you understand the objectives. It should be clear to you what the customer wants to achieve and your proposal and estimate of costs should now be a reflection of your Customer's Project Objectives. No less and no more.

Consider this: Why would you propose and/or cost anything other than what is required to *meet* your Customer's Project Objectives? In a competitive bid process, the customer can neither expect, nor does he or she expect, that his or her objectives will be exceeded. All the customer wants and can expect is for his or her objectives to be met at the best possible price.

3.1 Pricing the project

Now that you've determined that your proposal is going to be focused on meeting your Customer's Project Objectives, how are you going to price the project? This is an impossible question to answer unless you can prepare an accurate and reliable cost estimate — an estimate that takes into account *all* costs. Do not ever prepare a cost estimate on the basis of wishful thinking. Always base your cost estimates on proven cost data from your experience, from your documented historical costs, and from reliable sources of information. Any other method of estimating the cost of a project will be at your peril and ultimately will ensure that your Customer's Project Objectives will *not* be met, which is the last thing the customer wants. For example, if halfway through the project the Customer's Project Objectives are not being met, the lingering memory of your low price will long be forgotten and the only thing on the customer's mind will be: "How did I get into a position on my project where my objectives are not being met? This is a disaster." Do you know who the customer is going to blame? You! Welcome to "Small-Business Hell." Trust me, this is not a place you want to be.

Always keep in the forefront of your mind as you are trying to get the project that you must *build it for less than you sold it*. That's going to be a very tough task if you underestimate the cost of the project in the first place. Who is going to suffer along with you losing money on the project? The customer. You can be guaranteed that if you have underpriced the project that at some time throughout the project you are going to let down the customer and you are not going to meet all of the Customer's Project Objectives. Nobody ever wins when the contractor underprices the cost of the project.

What about your competition? Are they going to be doing exactly the same things as you? Maybe or maybe not. If your competitors read my book, maybe they are going to be doing the same as you. That is a better option than having your competitors in the marketplace selling to customers, to *your* customers and to your potential customers, at unrealistically low prices. We all know how these types of situations end. A bankrupt contractor, projects left incomplete, and the Customer's Project Objectives not met. Not a very good thing for our industry!

The next time one of your competitors puts in an unrealistically low price on a project in which you know they can't possibly make any money, mail them a copy of my book. If you can influence your competitors to be "good competitors," then you should do it. There is nothing worse in business than lousy competitors who always make their mark on the world by giving customers unrealistically low prices. You don't need this kind of competition, our industry doesn't need this kind of competition, and most certainly the customer doesn't need these kinds of competitors.

Whenever contractors put in an unrealistically low price they put the customer in a very difficult position. The customer can easily determine that one is less than two and the customer always wants to believe the lowest bidder. It is a much more difficult task for a customer to determine if a contractor, at the price provided, will meet all of his or her project objectives. Problem solved for the customer if all of the contractors have bid responsibly and all of the contractors have the ability to meet the Customer's Project Objectives. Unbelievable problems are just beginning for the customer if an irresponsible contractor provides the customer with an unrealistically low price and then cannot or does not meet all of the Customer's Project Objectives.

3.2 Getting the price right

The price you bid on a job has to include all your costs plus your profit. Remember, it is "sell for less than you can produce it," not the other way around. Typically your job costs fall into two categories:

- Cost of goods sold.

- Expenses (overhead).

Cost of goods sold are always on a per-job basis; therefore, when you are pricing a job you need to determine all costs that are going to be directly charged to the project. It is very easy to miss something in your bid. Be realistic, don't overestimate, and don't miss anything is the best advice I can give. The following is a list of things that should be considered as cost of goods sold:

- Material: All material incorporated into the project.

- Owned tools and equipment: A cost or an allowance for the tools you own that are required to complete the project.

- Rented tools and equipment: The costs of renting tools and equipment that you don't own.

- Expendables and supplies: Those little things that can add up to a lot if you miss them (e.g., tape, gloves, coveralls, cleaning supplies, nuts and bolts, shop supplies).

- Subcontractors: Bids from other contractors that are to be included in your bid.

- Labor: Direct labor costs for the project.

- Supervision: An allowance for supervision, if required.

- Indirect labor: Off-site support personnel.

- Overtime (if required).

- Travel time (if required).

- Other labor premiums.

- Safety supplies: An allowance for extraordinary safety requirements.

One very common question for small contractors is how should the labor costs for the owner be charged if the owner works directly on the job and does other non-job-specific, related tasks. The answer is that all time spent directly on a project should be charged to the project and the balance of the owner's labor costs should be charged to overhead.

Sample 6 is an example of a job-cost estimating sheet that could be used as a template for your estimate summary. You need to provide all the backup details to the estimate. (The download kit that comes with this book includes an MS Excel version of this sample.)

Job Cost Estimate

ABC Construction Company Job Cost Estimate
Project Name: New Windows Installed
Customer: XYZ Buildings

Cost Category	Estimated Cost
Material	5,000
Owned tools and equipment	500
Rented tools and equipment	500
Expendables and supplies	100
Subcontractors	2,000
Labor	5,000
Supervision	1,000
Indirect labor	500
Overtime allowance	500
Travel time allowance	250
Other labor premiums	250
Safety supplies	350
Sales taxes (included)	0
Total Cost	**$15,950**
Overhead percentage on cost (equal to 10% margin on selling price)	12.5%
Overhead cost	$1,994
Profit percentage on cost (equal to 10% margin on selling price)	12.5%
Profit	$1,994
Total Selling Price	**$19,938**

Note: Other sales taxes to be shown separately.

8
Produce It

You've sold it, now you have to produce it for less than you sold it, and you have to meet all of your Customer's Project Objectives.

This chapter will discuss "produce it," which means everything that takes place from the time the customer gives you the go-ahead, the contract, and/or the purchase order to the point in time where the project is complete.

A project has a defined start date and completion date. A project is similar to a vacation: There is the day you leave and the day you get back; what happens in between is the journey. You can have a great journey or the trip from hell; that's up to you. You know what your customer wants: A nice pleasant journey that runs on schedule, stays within budget, and meets all of the Customer's Project Objectives. You always want to be known as the contractor who will provide the best project journey for your customers; it's one of the main things that makes you unique compared to your competitors.

When your customer is making the choice as to which contractor to hire, you want to be the obvious choice. Your proposal offers your customer a commitment to schedule (Faster); a commitment to the customer's budget (Cheaper); and a quality project (Better). By implementing the Faster, Cheaper, Better (FCB) way, your customer can hopefully envision that a project journey with you will be far better than a project journey with your competitor. Every customer can determine that one is less than two but it takes an informed customer to be able to analyze bid proposals and select the best contractors for the project, not just based on price but based on FCB criteria and the projected journey.

1. Project Management

All of the tasks listed in this chapter are the responsibility of the project manager. This doesn't mean you have to hire a separate person to be your project manager. Project management means that for every project — small, medium, or large — there are certain tasks that must be undertaken to complete the project, and all of these tasks require a degree of management. In other words, *project tasks* need to be *managed* by a *project manager*.

You could be a one-person show and still have to manage the project; it's a necessary component of all successful projects. Let me rephrase that. Project management is optional if you don't want your project to succeed. The only differences between a project that is managed and one that is not managed are about one million things, and at the top of the list are two things that well-managed projects almost always achieve:

1. Profit for the contractor.

2. All the Customer's Project Objectives have been met.

Your choice is to manage your projects or not! The journey for you and your customer on a well-managed project will be enjoyable and profitable for both of you. The journey on a project that is not managed well can best be described as the trip from Hell!

Your primary objective as project manager is to efficiently and effectively manage all aspects of the project as defined. Your immediate response may be that you don't have time to look after all the project details. Efficient and effective project management returns many hours and many dollars in savings. You don't want to spend two hours on project management to save one hour in the field. That makes no sense at all. You do want to spend one hour on project management when there is the potential for savings in resources and to ensure that your Customer's Project Objectives are met.

Remember, this is what you need to accomplish:

- A commitment to meet *all* of your Customer's Defined Project Objectives for the project.

- A commitment to produce a project that is Faster, Cheaper, Better than the customer would have received if he or she had chosen any one of your competitors.

- The project was sold for $X and now you have to produce it for something less than $X.

What are the primary components of a successfully managed project? Let Faster, Cheaper, Better (FCB) be your guide. Subject every decision you are going to make on the project to this criteria.

There are an innumerable number of decisions that need to be made on every project by the project manager. To achieve a Faster, Cheaper, Better project, the very first place to start is to subject every decision you are going to make on the project to FCB criteria. This doesn't have to be some long-winded, pain-staking analysis you have to use your trained mind and project management experience to make project decisions that will produce FCB results.

For example: You have to choose a lead-hand or foreperson for the project. Who are you going to choose? What options do you have? By applying FCB criteria to your decision you are going to choose the individual that will achieve FCB results in the field.

Say your choice is between George and Jane.

George has a good long-term relationship with the customer. He completed an FCB training course that focused on teaching field personnel how to meet the Customer's Project Objectives in the field. George is available and has experience with this type of project. Given good project management support, George will meet the Customer's Project Objectives in the field.

Jane has not worked on a project with this customer before. She has not taken FCB training; however, Jane is available and is next in line to go to work. She will be angry if George is chosen over her. Jane needs more on-the-job training and experience to ensure she can meet the Customer's Project Objectives every time.

You choose. George is the best choice, obviously, even if Jane is going to be angry. The choice of the best lead-hand foreman or forewoman for the project is not a decision to be made lightly. Are you prepared to make the decision to put Jane in the position of lead-hand foreperson and put the project at risk of not meeting its project objectives? Or are you going to let FCB principles guide you and choose George for the project?

You know what you are going to do. You are going to choose George and you are going to use your project management skills to deal with Jane so she remains a good and faithful employee. You may be able to offer Jane an opportunity to work under George at a reduced rate to gain more experience until such time as a foreperson's job suited for her comes along.

Bottom line is, if you apply FCB principles to all your project decisions, you can't and won't make decisions that will put your Customer's Project Objectives at risk. You just won't. Following FCB principles and decision-making criteria needn't adversely affect schedule, cost, or quality. Following FCB principles will ensure Faster, Cheaper, Better results.

There are many books written about project management. You can get a degree in project management from many universities in North America. You can become accredited or earn a designation by the Project Management Institute, a not-for-profit organization with more than 650,000 members and certified credential holders in 185 countries. Why would you want to go down this road? Your objective as a small-business contractor is to efficiently and effectively manage projects in your area of expertise and projects of the size that fit within your overall business plan. You don't need a Project Management Professional designation, but you do need to understand the fundamentals of project management and how to apply them to your business.

2. Create a Project File

Create a project file that incorporates all of the information on the project. The Customer's Project Objectives can be defined in the "scope of work" section along with Faster, Cheaper, Better opportunities (see Sample 7). You will end up referring to the project file any number of times throughout the project so you will want to organize the project plan in a way that best suits your needs and offers ease of access for quick reference.

Are you going to keep your project plan in a hard copy or are you going to create a project plan on your laptop? You need to choose the method that best works for you.

If you are going to keep your plan on your computer, make sure you back up regularly, or keep electronic copies of your plan outside of your computer. Computers do crash on occasion and it is not a fun experience to lose an entire project file.

Project plans can vary from trade to trade but some of the information required is fundamental to all projects. For a hard copy plan I like to use a three-ring binder with numbered dividers. This way all project information is located in one easily accessible file. I then use a standard index that may be customized to any specific project.

3. Purchasing Materials

I refer to all supplies as material. For example, if you are a builder, materials may include concrete, steel, lumber, trusses, etc. Miscellaneous items that can be included under material are hardware, shop supplies, expendables, etc. The only items I typically don't include are those that are supplied and installed by others; this area I always refer to as subcontracts (quite often because sales taxes may be treated differently by material suppliers than subcontractors).

Requirements for purchasing material vary from trade to trade. Some trades provide a great deal of material and others much less so. Regardless of what category your business falls into, you can be guaranteed that if the material requirements for your project don't show up on time or aren't available, or they are more expensive than you allowed for in your estimate, or they don't meet the requirements of the project, you are going to have a problem on your hands. To avoid these challenges you need to work with your material suppliers and ensure that they will meet your project objectives.

How you purchase materials for your project is critical to the success of your project. You must take responsibility to ensure that you are communicating with your suppliers and that you have the information at hand to ensure that you are ordering the right

Sample 7
Project Plan

Project Name:
Customer:

Section	Description	Included in Each Section
1	Project Participants Contact List	Names, contact numbers, and email addresses of all project participants (including the customer) and what their roles are. You may have to add to this list as the project progresses.
2	Customer Details	Details about the customer and notes from whomever sold the project. Verbal orders are lost in space; make sure all information is conveyed from the seller to the project manager or person responsible for undertaking the project.
3	Scope of Work	Once a person has read the scope of work, he or she will know about the project, what is included and excluded, what the Customer's Project Objectives are, and other specific project information. A schedule can be included in this section or you can create a separate section for schedules that are more detailed.
4	Budget and Job Cost Reports	This section should include project budget, contract details, contract amount, column for contract revisions, cost allocations by code, and projected gross profit. Job cost reports can be more detailed with allowances for various cost codes depending on how much information is required for the project manager to effectively manage the project.
5	Contract or Purchase Order	A copy of the contract, purchase order, or signed authorization from the customer.
6	Invoicing Details	Information for the bookkeeper on how to invoice the customer, terms and conditions of payment, etc.
7	Material Suppliers	Information on material suppliers for the project including quotes, contracts, and scopes of supply. On larger projects this section will be expanded.
8	Subcontractors	If you will be engaging subcontractors, this section should include their scope of work, contracts, terms of payment, etc. You should also advise all subcontractors on how you expect them to invoice your business and your terms and conditions unless they are defined in your contract with the subcontractor.
9	Other	Other information that you want included in the project book.

supplies. Are you going to use a purchase order system to authorize material purchases? If so, how are you going to manage this? You can buy purchase order books at your local stationery store. See Sample 8 for an example of a purchase order.

If you do use a purchase order (PO) system, you should list the materials purchased on the PO, the price, the job number, and coding. When the supplier invoice arrives it can then be matched to the PO for accuracy. On larger projects or remote projects that you can't control directly you should have a delivery slip or packing slip signed on receipt of the materials and this can be matched to the invoice as well (be sure to record any damage on the delivery slip). On the PO you can check to make sure what you have been billed for is what you bought and that the price is correct.

Using the matching delivery slip you can check to make sure the materials were received in good order.

On some projects you may have a quote from your suppliers for a specific list of project materials, in which case you will want to choose a supplier that meets your objectives.

Here's an example: You need to order all of the major material for the project. The lowest bidder for the major material has a reputation of being notoriously late with deliveries and many times goods arrive damaged. By choosing this supplier, you are going to put the project at risk of not meeting its project objectives, but the project cannot afford the additional costs of going with the second lowest bid for major material supply. What should you do? Apply the Faster, Cheaper, Better principles. Meet with the supplier and its key personnel or contacts in the supply chain and openly discuss the challenges and the risks that you would be taking if you award the company the project. You are not going to put your Customer's Project Objectives at risk under any circumstances. Describe what the supplier can do to ensure that your Customer's Project Objectives are met.

About 99 times out of 100 when a supplier doesn't perform it's because it doesn't know and understand what your project objectives are and, consequently, how you are dependent on the supplier to ensure that you can meet your Customer's Project Objectives. After talking to the supplier, you may be pleasantly surprised that your supplier eagerly responds to your requests and commits to put in place the necessary procedures to ensure that it meets your specified project objectives. After all, your supplier wants to build a good relationship with your company and the best way to do that is to do business with you and meet your project objectives every time.

4. Contract Administration

You are bound to a contract whether it is by handshake, purchase order, or written contract. You have agreed to undertake a scope of work and agreed to a price or a schedule of costs to complete the work. Does that mean you never have to refer to the contract again? No, that's not the right attitude.

The contract may define, or you may have verbally agreed to, a number of contract administration matters (e.g., how to invoice a customer, when to invoice a customer, invoice backup, proof of

Purchase Order

ABC Construction Company

Date:
Supplier: XYZ Supply Company
Address:
Contact name:
Contact number:
Contact email:
PO number: 1001- 985 *(Job number followed by sequential PO number.)*

Please provide the following per the terms and conditions herein:

Supply	Quantity	Unit Price	Total
Units of lumber	1,000	15	15,000

Deliver: to ABC Construction Company at the Smith Building
Tag: Job number 1001 lumber
Attention:

Terms and Conditions
(You can insert terms and conditions negotiated with the supplier.)
Delivery date on site:
Packaging requirements:
Labeling requirements:
Notification prior to delivery:

statutory payments, reporting criteria). The contract administration documents and requirements for the project need to be defined and you need to adhere them. There is nothing worse than when you send your first invoice and you expect to be paid within two weeks but instead are advised you did not follow the contract in how to prepare your invoice and the client is holding the payment until you get it right. Now you get paid in 60 days instead of 14 days. Explain that to your banker.

To avoid any issues in the area of contract administration, be sure you know what you are agreeing to under the terms of the contract. If the customer doesn't define the terms and conditions, you should define them under the terms of your proposal and scope of work. Then ensure that the contract requirements are adhered to. Verbal agreements are easily lost, especially in this area. Make sure terms and conditions are written down and agreed upon.

Contracts for projects not only concern the project manager but your bookkeeper and/or accountant as well. Contracts may state a number of commercial requirements that must be complied with and, typically, if these requirements are not complied with, you will be penalized or your invoices won't be paid. The project manager needs to review the contracts in their entirety and highlight all clauses that may impact contract administration, and then bring all of these requirements and information to the attention of the bookkeeper or accountant.

5. Construction Management

Isn't construction management the same as project management? No. Construction management is a part of the project management process but focuses on the actual construction component of the project. You can define within your own organization what you consider to be construction management versus project management. The reason to separate the two is to ensure there is a focus on the field or shop component of the project as this is typically your primary source of costs and risk.

When construction management and project management are separated, these types of tasks could be the responsibility of the construction manager:

- Management and overseeing of site personnel.

- Receipt of materials and equipment on-site and management of materials on-site pending installation.

- Coordination of day-to-day construction activities on-site.

- Management of information and drawings on-site (you don't want to provide crews with out-of-date information or drawings because you may have to redo the job at your expense).

- Communication and coordination on-site with the customer and other project participants.

- Ensuring that the required tools are on the project, in good operating condition, when they are required.

6. Customer Relations

Rumor has it that a big department store had an unwritten rule with its customers: "They don't talk to us and we don't talk to them." This company went broke and lack of communication is probably the main reason why. You need to maintain a good relationship with your customers and practice good communications.

There may be times when you think this is impossible but if you don't retain a good working relationship with your customers, the project journey can quickly go from a love-in to an unworkable and untenable situation. No one wants to have a bad relationship with a customer and sometimes it may take an extraordinary effort with a difficult customer, but in the end a good relationship will be far better than a relationship that has deteriorated to the point in which the customer doesn't want to pay you. If that ever happens, you will wish that you had spent a little more effort in maintaining a good relationship with the customer. These are the keys to ensuring a good relationship with your customer:

- Communicate with your clients.

- Keep your clients informed of any potential changes and potential change in cost *before* costs are incurred. Never surprise your customers.

- Clear and concise scope of work and clearly defined Customers' Project Objectives.

- Be committed. The customers know that you and your team are committed to the project and to meeting their project objectives.

- Lead the project. You are the leader on the project and by your very leadership other project participants are meeting their objectives. You must remain a positive influence on the entire project.

- Be honest with your customers.

I can't say it enough how important it is to have efficient and effective communication with all project participants and suppliers with whom you need to interact. By clearly communicating your project needs and schedule requirements, everyone knows where you are coming from. You have given them the opportunity to lead, follow, or get the hell out of your way!

7. Scheduling

You need to decide who is setting the project schedule. This could be you, the customer, or some other project participant. Whoever is responsible, a realistic, achievable project schedule must be created, communicated, updated, and adhered to by all project participants.

Scheduling can be as simple as setting a date for when the project must be complete all the way up to scheduling specific components of a project, relationships amongst the various project components and participants, and setting progress milestones. I have worked with schedulers who have doctorate degrees and schedulers who gave me a single date to be complete.

The biggest scheduling challenges are due to the interrelationships that exist on site. Contractor B can't start his work until contractor A completes his work. If Contractor A is late, then Contractor B will be late. Who is then responsible for the project delay? If Contractor B has to accelerate his work at additional cost, who is responsible? The complexities of scheduling can be overwhelming if not managed properly. Entire books are written about the scheduling process so there isn't enough room in this book to get into too much detail. A few basic scheduling fundamentals are as follows:

- You or some other project participant must take responsibility for the overall project schedule.

- All critical project participants must have input into the schedule.

- Each project participant should create his or her own schedule that can be integrated into the overall schedule.

- Relationships and dependencies amongst project participants must be identified.

- Schedules must be realistic, achievable, and have buy-in from all critical project participants.

- Project participants must be prepared to commit to their responsibilities defined in the schedule. If they can't, the entire schedule could be in jeopardy.

- Are there going to be penalties and/or consequences for project participants who don't meet their schedule obligations?

- Allowances need to be made, or at least there needs to be agreement and acknowledgment as to what will happen in the case of weather delays and other unforeseen circumstances.

- Good Faster, Cheaper, Better contractors will be easily identified on-site as the contractors who are on schedule, who lead by example, and who communicate all schedule interrelationships that could jeopardize their ability to meet their schedule commitments.

There are a number of project management and scheduling programs available for more complex projects. The complexity of the project should define the complexity of the schedule. On most simple projects a single straight line on the schedule with a defined start date and finish date will suffice. One project participant though, likely the overall project manager, needs to ensure that all project participants are held to account for their project responsibilities. Communicate, remind, and seek commitment. That is a good way to manage a schedule.

Project participants who do not meet their schedule commitments must be taken to task and become willing participants in meeting the overall scheduled objectives. There will always be challenges, late deliveries, and contractors who don't live up to their scheduled commitments. These project participants must be encouraged to become part of the solution and not part of the problem. Failing success on this, other more drastic courses of action may be required such as monetary penalties, delay in payment of invoices, being stricken from the list of contractors eligible to participate in the next project, and flogging — no, not flogging, we are not allowed to do that anymore!

8. Managing Resources

Every project requires resources. Typically all project resources will fall into one of the following categories:

- Labor.

- Materials.

- Equipment.

- Tools.

- Information.

- Clear and concise direction.

Resources need to be available on the job, when required and organized for specific project tasks. In your particular field of expertise, you know how to manage and organize resources in order to ensure that the field labor can work as efficiently and effectively as possible. You also know, from your experience, what not to do. The following basic rules apply to almost any project situation:

- Organize and manage project resources so that they are readily available when and where required. Don't be one of those contractors where the field personnel spend 50 percent of their time looking for something or waiting for supplies to be delivered because someone forgot to order them. The project manager or construction manager must take responsibility for managing resources and this takes organization.

- Project hardware is typically inexpensive. Don't let a lack of it, or poorly managed project hardware, be the excuse for poor efficiency on your project. Site foreperson: "Don't blame me boss, I can't find it; it's not here." Boss: "Well, look again." Site foreperson later that day: "OK we found it; someone put it on the site and it was hidden behind a bunch of other material." Boss: "OK, that's great, but we've lost an entire day and now we have to make it up somehow." How many times have you heard this conversation?

- Tools need to be in good working condition and, if required, support resources such as power, oil, and fuel need to be readily available. There is nothing worse than a five-person crew waiting around because the equipment ran out of gas. That will not produce Faster, Cheaper, Better results.

- Within your project schedule, ensure equipment and heavy materials arrive on site when you need them. Repeated moves of equipment and materials will inevitably cause damage and cost money on the project. If material arrives on the site too early, you are creating opportunities for the material to get damaged, stolen, or lost.

- Field personnel need information. Provide the required information in bite-sized pieces in easily accessible information packages. Don't send 100 pages of documents to the field when they only need 10. You'll just be paying your field personnel time to search through a maze of information that they don't need in order to find the information they do need.

- Clear and concise direction means just that. Communicate clearly with your field personnel so that they know what your expectations are. Communicating your expectations may open discussions on how your expectations can be achieved. If you don't provide clear and concise direction, don't expect your field personnel to be able to read your mind.

9. Mobilizing

Mobilizing sounds simple, but it is a critical part of the project. Ensure your project starts out on the right foot. You never get a second chance to make a first impression.

Mobilizing means organizing everything you need to do prior to the first day on the job and then commencing operations on the job. Everything you forget to do in the mobilization stage will cost many more times to do after the job has started. Prior to anyone starting work on-site there is usually an opportunity of time for you to plan the project. The following are some of the mobilization things you need to think:

- Material and equipment deliveries required on the first day on the job.

- Labor and crew plan.

- Supervisor orientation and introduction to the project, scope of work, and Customer's Project Objectives.

- Coordination and introduction to other site personnel and project participants.

- Arrangement for site storage, laydown area, office trailer (if required), site security, and access.

- Schedule review.

- Invoicing, job costing, and reporting requirements review with the bookkeeper or billing clerk.

There may be a number of other things you should do prior to and on day one. Requirements vary from contractor to contractor. The key point is that you should use this period of time to set the project in motion on the right foot. A project that starts well has a much better opportunity to finish well than a project that has a rough and disorganized mobilization.

10. Supervising

Supervisors need to provide clear and concise direction to field crews. A two-person crew still typically needs one person to be the leader and give direction. Good supervisory skills include the following traits:

- Leadership.

- Trust.

- Knowledge.

- Organization.

- Communication.

- Reliability.

- Fairness.

- Respect.

- Demanding (within reason).

- Objective-oriented.

Supervisory skill training within your organization will prove to be a good investment. Your expectations for your supervisors should be clearly communicated to them; they need to be trained, they need to buy into your expectations, and all supervisors need to understand that when they are on-site they are representing you and your business and anything less than your expectations being met will not be accepted or tolerated.

Long gone are the days of supervisors using intimidation, bullying, and belittling of employees to try to achieve their objectives. Good supervisors are leaders and command respect because of who they are and how they act. They earn respect from those they supervise and they get that respect by how they lead and treat their crew. Good supervisors promote good morale on site, good relationships among site personnel, provide great leadership, lead by example, and are the people on-site other project participants look up to and on whom they rely. Poor leadership results in poor morale, which translates into a poor job done and project objectives not being met. Faster, Cheaper, Better objectives will never be met with poor project supervision — that is a guarantee.

11. Quality Control

Quality is all about the *better* in Faster, Cheaper, Better (FCB). Remember it is not the *best*; it is *better*, which is defined in the project scope of work and the Customer's Project Objectives.

You need to meet the quality objectives as defined. For example, you have sold the customer a project with a defined quality standard and if you exceed that standard, the customer may thank you but he or she isn't going to pay you more money.

Almost everything we buy is graded or has a level of quality. If we want a higher quality, we will have to pay more money. We don't expect to pay for C grade and have A grade delivered. The same goes in our business. You need to define the quality objectives and then meet them. Of course, it is very important that the customer knows and understands what he or she is getting. There is nothing worse than the customer expecting one thing and you delivering something different. That will make your FCB objectives fly out the window faster than anything.

12. Demobilization

Your last hurrah on the site; make it a good one. Back at the mobilization stage you only had one chance to make a first impression. The same applies at the demobilization stage; make sure all the good things you have done on the project are backed up by a well-managed, well-executed, and timely demobilization. The customer will always remember your last day on-site.

Think about these key demobilization tasks:

- Material and equipment removed from the site.

- Site clean-up in areas of your responsibility.

- Communication and coordination with remaining site personnel.

- Final checklist before leaving site and signoff where required.

- Ensure that only your materials and equipment are removed from the site; there is nothing worse than packing up another contractor's gear by mistake.

- Final review: Make sure all of your Customer's Project Objectives have been met.

- Conduct a walk-through with the customer.

- Final invoicing, job costing, and reporting requirements complete.

- Agreement on any deficiencies (must be documented in writing) and when and how they will be addressed.

13. Contract Wrap-up

As the old saying goes, no job is done until the paperwork is complete. This applies to your contract as well as final billing, as-built drawings, confirmation of statutory requirements, warranty certificates, and any other items required by the scope of work and Customer's Project Objectives. Don't be the last contractor to get the contract wrapped up; be the first. At this stage, the customer's only handle over you is the money you are owed. Don't give your customer any excuse not to pay you on time.

9
Account for It

First, you have to *sell it*; second, you have to *produce it for less than you sold it*; and third, you have to *account for it*. This chapter will provide you with what you need to know about accounting for it and all the related paperwork. This chapter includes samples that are also available in the download kit so you can print or save the forms and use them to help you keep organized in your business.

The paper trail in your business will be long and complex and must be managed. Sample 9 is an example of a paper trail for a single project in a typical business in our industry. You may require more or less information to efficiently and effectively manage your business.

Now that you have had an introduction to the contract administration requirements for a typical project you will need to decide who is going to be responsible for these tasks in your business.

1. Hire Someone to Help You

If you are a typical small-business person not trained as an accountant or a bookkeeper, the list of accounting requirements

Paper Trail for Projects and Related Accounting Requirements

Business Development	Faster, Cheaper, Better Sample Reference Documents
Project estimate and all related backup information and correspondence.	• Project estimate sheet and project estimate summary.
Project scope of work, proposal, and Customer's Project Objectives.	• Proposal documents and contract acceptance.

Project Manager Project File	Faster, Cheaper, Better Sample Reference Documents
Copies of all project related information.	
Purchase orders for material and equipment.	• Purchase order (see Chapter 8, Sample 8).
Labor time sheets with coding.	• Time sheet (form included in download kit).
Contract change orders.	• Change order.

Project Bookkeeping and Job Cost Records	Faster, Cheaper, Better Sample Reference Documents
Billing information sheet (clear and concise direction to the bookkeeper on all required information including billing procedures, budget, and job-cost requirements).	
Job-cost report summarizing costs to date on a project.	• Job-cost report.
Customer invoicing.	• Invoice.

Business Bookkeeping and Accounting	Faster, Cheaper, Better Sample Reference Documents
Work in progress.	• Work-in-progress calculation sheet
Balance sheet.	• See Chapter 3, Sample 2.
Statement of Earnings and Retained Earnings.	• See Chapter 3, Sample 1.

for your company should be enough to give you a headache. If you are trained as an accountant or a bookkeeper, you know and understand the meaning of all of these requirements. In order to be successful in business, you have to be adept at accounting and bookkeeping or you need to have a good working knowledge of all of the requirements. You may need to hire an accountant or a bookkeeper who is adept at accounting functions if you are not.

Let's assume that you are not a trained accountant or book-keeper and you are going to hire someone to perform the accounting function in your company. This means that you still have to have a good working knowledge of all of these accounting requirements. How are you going to acquire this knowledge? The best advice is to take accounting courses, attend accounting training sessions, and read accounting-related books at the same time that you are learning the technical side of your industry. Remember you are not trying to become an accountant, that could take a number of years, but you are acquiring enough knowledge in all aspects of the accounting function in your company so you know what your accountant, bookkeeper, and lawyer are talking about and so that you can give meaningful direction in this regard.

Typically a bookkeeper, either hired directly or under contract, can prepare monthly financial statements to meet your specific needs. The key is to know and understand how to read these financial statements so you can ask questions to better understand your financial position. Of course, it is extremely important for you to subject the financial statements to your own review to ensure that your bookkeeper is keeping and preparing accurate and reliable accounting information. Bookkeepers are not created equal so hopefully you have engaged a good one. If not, you could be headed towards accounting Hell; trust me, you don't want to go there.

In the beginning ask your accountant to review your bookkeeper's work to ensure that you have engaged the best. Misleading financial information could result in you believing you are doing well when in fact you are losing money. This is a surefire way to go broke.

All accounting can be done by computer program today and with your accountant's advice you can choose the program that is best suited to your business. Accounting programs, like bookkeepers, are not created equal and you need a program that is very good at job costing for multiple projects and one that lets you create job cost codes that will meet your specific job costing requirements.

2. Invoicing and Collections

Invoicing and collections is an area in which a business can get into a lot of trouble if not managed properly. For example, poor billing practices will give your customer an excuse to not pay you on time. All of your financial commitments are dependent on billing your customers and collecting your receivables on time. This starts with good billing practices, invoicing to your customer's defined requirements, and insisting that you be paid on time in accordance with the terms and conditions you defined with your customer in the "sell it" phase.

Note that customers may have specific coding functions and invoicing requirements that you must comply with and it's far better to get these defined up front rather than at the eleventh hour when you are waiting to be paid.

Before entering into contracts with any customers, and providing them with credit, you should have your potential customers complete a credit application. You will be filling out applications yourself when applying for credit with your suppliers so it is only fair that your customers complete one for your business. Granting of credit to customers is no different than you lending them money. You know a bank isn't going to lend you money without an application and provision of credit information, so you shouldn't be expected to grant credit to your customers unless they are willing to undergo a credit review prior to you granting them credit.

There are exceptions to every rule, and if you are dealing with someone you know or a very reputable company, you may want to forgo this procedure. If you are bidding on major capital projects, you will also want to investigate who is providing the financing and ensure that your customer's financing is secure.

If a customer doesn't pay in accordance with agreed-on terms and conditions, what do you do? First of all, don't wait and assume everything is okay; communicate with your customer and get to the bottom of the problem. You have entered into a contract and you expect your customer to honor his or her commitment and this must be communicated clearly to your customer. If payment is not forthcoming, you will have to investigate builders' liens, legal action, or other methods of collection. Remember, for every dollar you don't collect from a bad, non-paying customer you will have to do $20 of work for good, paying customers just to break even.

The best remedy for this problem is due diligence prior to entering into a contract with your customer. If your customer is extremely belligerent or difficult when it comes to credit terms, maybe you should forget this customer and move onto customers who you have more confidence in. Even good customers can get themselves into difficulty at times so be aware.

See Sample 10 for a basic invoice sample. (Note there is a version of this sample included in the download kit, which you can customize to use for your business.)

Invoice

Company Name: *ABC Construction Company*
Address: *123 ABC Street, Anywhere, Zip/Postal Code*

Sold To: *Customer's name*
Customer's address:

Project: *Name of Project*
Description: *Project Description*

Customer Order Number:
Order Date:
Job Number:
Invoice Date:
Invoice Number:

Description
Full description of what this invoice is for and a breakdown of the amount being invoiced.

Typical invoicing options:

Time and Material
Provide a list of labor, material, and other billable items with quantities, unit prices, and total price for each item.

Fixed Contract Amount without a Holdback Billed by Percentage Complete

Contract Amount	$10,000	
Percentage Complete		50%
Value of Work Completed	$5,000	
Previously Invoiced		$2,000
This Invoice		$3,000
Tax 1 (if applicable)		
Tax 2 (if applicable)		
Total Due		**$3,000**

Fixed Contract Amount with a Holdback Billed by Percentage Complete

Contract Amount	$10,000	
Percentage Complete		50%
Value of Work Completed	$5,000	
Less 10% Holdback		$500
Less Previously Invoiced	$1,800	
This Invoice		$2,700
Tax 1 (if applicable)		
Tax 2 (if applicable)		
Total Due		**$2,700**

Attachments to the invoice could include:

- Backup for labor, material, and other items being invoiced.

- Customer sign-off sheets.

- Statutory declarations stating that you have paid your labor and material suppliers to date.

- Other declarations that may be required by your customer.

Other invoice details that should be on the invoice:

- Payment terms (e.g., "payment due upon receipt of invoice").

- Late payment terms: (e.g., interest will be charged at 1.75% (23.14% per annum) on accounts not paid within 30 days of invoice date).

- Tax registration and other license numbers required in your jurisdiction.

3. General Accounting

For general accounting you will want to use one of the common accounting programs that are available online or from stationery stores. These programs have different features and one may be better suited to your business than the other. Every bookkeeper today uses one or more of these programs and as you are doing your investigation into bookkeepers you can investigate the best accounting software for your business.

Do not agree to any form of custom software or nontraditional software programs. You will live to regret it after you've wasted thousands of dollars. Stick to the standard programs that are available, and to bookkeepers who are familiar with these programs. Job costing for a contractor is a key feature of some programs, so if you envision that you will be using the job costing feature, make sure that your bookkeeper is familiar with these requirements.

If your plan is to not hire a bookkeeper, be prepared to go to night school to learn the program of your choice. All good accounting programs provide all aspects of general accounting including payroll, accounts receivable, accounts payable, cheques and payments, etc. Most programs will provide additional software to allow your accounting program to do payroll and deal with federal, state or provincial, and local payroll taxes.

4. Banking

How much money do you need to operate your business? That certainly depends on what kind of business you have: Payment terms and conditions from your customer, payment terms with your suppliers, and other commitments and requirements. The key is you don't want to be overexposed to debt. Your accountant can advise you in this regard but a good rule of thumb is you should have one dollar in equity for every dollar in debt you take on.

How do you start your business when you have limited capital to invest in your business? Start small and build your business on retained earnings. There are also the options of applying for a line of credit, capital bank loan, and mortgage:

- **Line of credit:** An agreement with your bank to allow you to overdraw your account by an agreed-on maximum amount. The line of debits and credits can be handled automatically by your bank to save you from having to manage it on a daily basis. Be aware that the agreed-on line of credit may be subject to margin requirements and other conditions as discussed below.

- **Capital bank loans:** Used for acquiring equipment and other large capital expenditures. These loans come with specific terms and conditions and the lender will usually secure these loans with security agreements and similar documents. You can talk to your banker or lender about these types of loans.

- **Mortgages:** Typically these are for real estate acquisitions. Commercial mortgages can have different terms and conditions than residential mortgages so make sure you are aware of all the terms and conditions before agreeing to a loan of this nature.

- **Margin and other loan commitment requirements:** Your bank or lender will want the loans secured in a number of ways. You can expect your bank or lender to provide you with a sheet outlining terms and conditions for your loan. In the case of a revolving line of credit, you may need to meet certain margin and other requirements in order to access your loan. For example, your lender may only allow you to draw your line of credit to a maximum of 75 percent of your current accounts receivable; therefore, you can only margin your accounts receivable to 75 percent.

Every business needs a bank and an account representative with some degree of knowledge about your business and banking requirements. If you are operating on your own financial strength and you don't need a line of credit or overdraft protection, good for you! However, if you are like most businesses, you will need a line of credit from your bank to accommodate your business's financial commitments.

Your bank is in business to make money and the best way it can do that is to deal with good customers it knows are financially secure and will be able to repay any debt. Your bank is not prepared to take all the risks; it expects you to put money into your business and possibly to provide personal guarantees for any loans that it makes to your company. Your bank will always be more than happy to deal with you as long as you are making money and fulfilling your commitments to the bank. If you are in default, don't expect a lot of sympathy from your bank. Make money, retain your profits, and fulfill your commitments so everything will be good.

The bank will also expect you to provide accounting information on a regular basis; your bank will provide you with its requirements. Usually this includes monthly reports that would include in-house prepared financial statements, accounts receivable, payable listings, and work-in-progress reports. Annual reporting would include financial statements that may need to be prepared by your accountant.

Personal guarantees are your bank's way of attaining additional security and assuring that you are really committed to the success of your business. As soon as you sign a personal guarantee you have put a lot more on the line than you may think. Stack up a bunch of personal guarantees from your bank, leasing company, and major suppliers and you are more than committed, you have put all of your personal assets at risk. This is the tipping point for many entrepreneurs and the point at which you may be putting the well-being of your family at risk as well.

Your personal guarantee may involve your spouse or partner and he or she may have to sign a guarantee as well. If this is the case, the bank may require him or her to seek independent legal advice so he or she is advised of the risks of signing a personal guarantee, without you being in the room.

Personal guarantees signed by you and your spouse is a huge commitment from not just you but your entire family. Personal guarantees can be reduced or eliminated if your borrowing requirements are small. Instead of growing your business with bank debt, grow your business with retained earnings. If you believe the risk of taking on a higher level of debt is to your benefit because you can take on more work, then be fully aware of the consequences if anything goes wrong in your business.

5. Job Costing

Accurate and reliable job-cost reports are important for you to successfully manage your projects and your business. They are also mandatory; the alternative is management by wishful thinking in which you think things are going along just great when in fact you are losing money on a project. Job-cost reports should be prepared at least monthly or more often for every active project in order to calculate work in progress which is an integral part of your monthly financial statements.

Job-cost reports can be printed directly from your accounting program, or you may want to consider creating a custom job-cost report prepared in Excel and then download job cost data from your accounting program to the MS Excel program. Creating your own Excel job cost report can give you a great deal of flexibility in how to format your reports and you can create all of these reports in-house with the assistance of your bookkeeper. If your bookkeeper can't help you create your job costs reports in Excel, you have hired the wrong bookkeeper; it's time for an upgrade. (Note that the download kit includes a job cost report template that you can customize to fit your business.)

A job cost report typically has the following information (see Sample 11):

- Detailed project information: Include all project information that you believe is pertinent to the report that will assist you when you are reviewing the report.

- Job cost codes or categories: Codes that may include a designation showing cost type such as labor, material, equipment, expenses, subcontracts, and code number. You can use descriptions, categories, or create custom account numbers for your project. All good cost-accounting programs can accommodate your needs in this regard.

- Original estimated cost: Estimated cost from the original project cost estimate.

- Change orders: Include all revisions to date that amend the original cost budget and contract amount. (There is a blank version of this form included in the download kit.)

- Revised cost estimate: Includes the original estimate plus all change orders.

- Cost to date: Total of all actual recorded costs to date for each code or category.

- Estimated cost to complete: Estimated cost to complete the project; this is not a mathematical process but an actual prepared estimate of the cost to complete the project.

- Projected cost at completion: Projected final cost for each code or category.

- Projected over or under (-): A projection of where the costs for this code will end up at the end of the project. This is your first indication as to whether your project is trending towards being completed, under, or over budget. Remember on all contract jobs the money you save ends up in your pocket, and the excess money you spend comes from your project net profit or out of your pocket.

- Detailed summary information: This is shown at the bottom of the report, which includes sums of the various columns, revenue projections, gross profit estimates, and gross profit percentage projections.

5.1 Estimated cost to complete

The estimated cost to complete the project is not "estimated project costs minus costs to date." The estimated cost to complete is an accurate and reliable estimate of the costs to complete the project prepared by the project manager every time a job cost report is prepared.

You will see in Sample 11 that the estimated cost to complete (see sixth column) is a number that in the real world has been estimated by the project manager. In the sample report it looks like some costs are going to be higher and some costs lower than estimated, but overall the project looks like it will come in on or under budget and at this time the report is predicting that the project is going to make more money than estimated. A good position to be in if this report was reality and not fiction.

Estimated cost to complete is very easy to calculate at two times throughout a project; when the project is 0 percent complete and when the project is 100 percent complete. Every time, in between 0 and 100 percent, the cost to complete is just an estimate but an estimate that you are relying on in order to prepare accurate and reliable job cost report information.

To create an accurate and reliable estimated cost to complete you need to create your estimate in accordance with cost codes on the job cost report. How are actual costs coming in versus estimated project costs? Are costs trending higher, the same as, or lower than what you estimated. This is vital information if you are going to create an accurate and reliable estimated cost to complete.

It is the project manager's responsibility to fully understand all aspects of the job-cost report and to prepare an accurate and a reliable cost to complete estimate for each cost category at regular periods throughout the project. Professional project managers don't manage their projects based on management by wishful thinking, they manage their projects based on factual information and they are constantly striving to meet or better job cost estimates.

Sample 12 will give you a better understanding of an Estimate Sheet.

5.2 Projected over or under

Projected over or under between the final budget and projected final is critical information. If the variance is zero, you are saying that the project costs will come in on budget. If the variance indicates lower project costs, you are anticipating higher gross profits on the project than estimated. If the variance indicates higher project costs, you are anticipating lower gross profits or even a loss on the project. What are you going to do with this information?

Job Cost Report

Company: *ABC Construction Company*
Job No.: *1001*
Project name: *Smith Building*
As at date: *July 1, 20--*

Estimate Summary

Cost Category	Original Estimated Cost	Change Order No. 1	Revised Estimate Cost	Cost to Date	Estimated Cost to Complete	Projected Cost at Completion	Projected Over or Under (-) Estimate
Material	$23,950	$5,000	$28,950	$12,000	$17,155	$29,155	$205
Owned tools and equipment	$5,000		$5,000	$2,000	$3,000	$5,000	
Rented tools and equipment	$4,000		$4,000	$1,000	$2,580	$3,580	-$420
Expendables and supplies	$2,000	$200	$2,200	$1,000	$1,200	$2,200	
Subcontractors	$12,645		$12,645	$8,000	$4,645	$12,645	
Labor	$9,555	$2,345	$11,900	$5,000	$6,500	$11,500	-$400
Supervision	$1,000	$200	$1,200	$500	$400	$900	-$300
Indirect labor	$500	$100	$600	$200	$500	$700	$100
Overtime allowance	$500	$50	$550	$100	$250	$350	-$200
Travel time allowance	$250		$250		$250	$250	
Other labor premiums	$250		$250		$250	$250	
Safety supplies	$350	$105	$455	$200	$255	$455	
Sales taxes (not included)							
Total Estimated Cost	$60,000	$8,000	$68,000	$30,000	$36,985	$66,985	-$1,015

Gross Profit	$15,000	$2,000	$17,000

Contract Price	$75,000	$10,000	$85,000

Sample 12
Estimate Sheet

Company name: *ABC Construction Company*
Project name: *Smith Building*
Estimate No: *E115*

Estimate Takeoff

Item	Unit Quantity	Price per Unit	Total Price	Labor Hours per Unit	Total Hours
Concrete	24	$100	$2,400	2	48
Piping	100	$10	$1,000	0.5	50
Lumber	1,000	$15	$15,000	0.1	100
Steel	75	$74	$5,500	1	75
Total			**$23,950**		**273**

Labor Summary

Labor Hours from Estimate	Total
Hours	273
Hourly rate cost*	$35.00
Total labor cost	$9,555.00

*Hourly rate cost includes all labor-related costs (e.g., payroll taxes, holiday pay).

Estimate Summary

Cost Category	Estimated Cost
Material	$23,950
Owned tools and equipment	$5,000
Rented tools and equipment	$4,000
Expendables and supplies	$2,000
Subcontractors	$12,645
Labor	$9,555
Supervision	$1,000
Indirect labor	$500
Overtime allowance	$500
Travel time allowance	$250
Other labor premiums	$250
Safety supplies	$350
Sales taxes (not included)	
Total Estimated Cost	**$60,000**

Overhead percentage	12.5%
Overhead cost	$7,500

Profit percentage	12.5%
Profit	$7,500

Gross Profit (overhead + profit)	**$15,000**

Total Estimated Selling Price	**$75,000**
Bid Price	**$75,000**

Note: Other sales taxes to be shown separately.

If gross profits are indicating they will be higher, it would appear that the project is going to be a success. If the project is on budget, that's good. If the variance indicates higher project costs than estimated, you have a problem. Why? Was your estimate too low? Have on-site conditions changed causing increased costs? The project manager needs to investigate and determine why the project costs are trending higher and what can be done to correct the situation.

I am a believer that you should be able to create an accurate and reliable cost-to-complete estimate when the project is somewhere between 25 and 35 percent complete. At this stage, you should have enough project experience and information to know how estimated costs are trending. Also, the project is at an early enough stage that you may have the opportunity to do something about the problem. Are there site conditions that are causing extra costs that could be recouped with a change order? Are your field personnel best suited for the project? Are there some other underlying problems? If this is a cost-plus project with a budget, and the job cost record is indicating that the project is going to go over budget, you need to advise your customer *now*. Customers hate surprises more than anything else. You need to communicate with your customer. At the project completion stage when it is 25 to 35 percent complete, it is still early enough for you to have an opportunity to do something about it if your project has a problem. After 35 percent done, opportunities quickly disappear.

Please take the time to really understand work-in-progress calculations, because misunderstanding can lead to some problems. Work-in-progress is a mathematical calculation based on project data:

Gross profit percentage estimate calculation = Revised gross profit estimate X 100

Revised contract or budget

A contract summary report is a summary report that includes all contracts in progress and is a concise report that provides an overview of all projects. The contract summary will often bring attention to a particular project that may have issues. If there are issues, you can go to the actual job cost report for the project to look at more detailed information. Typically the following information is included:

- Project description: Job name and number and a notation as to the contract type.

- Project manager: All the project managers' initials if there is more than one in your company.

- Completion date: Month.

- Contract price or budget: In the case of cost-plus or cost reimbursable projects.

- Revised contract price: Include all revisions to date.

- Cost to date: Recorded costs to date from your job cost accounting system.

- Cost to complete: An estimate to be completed by the project manager.

- Billed to date: Sum of all invoices issued to date.

- Billings received: Sum of all payments received to date.

- Billings due: Billed to date minus billings received.

- Work in progress: Cost to date plus profit earned to date minus billed to date. A negative work in progress is an overbilling and a positive work in progress is an underbilling.

- Profit earned to date: Cost to date ÷ (cost to date + cost to complete) X (revised gross profit forecast). Essentially cost to date ÷ (cost to date + cost to complete) = percentage complete. For example, if the project is 50 percent complete, you have earned 50 percent of the revised gross profit forecast.

- Original gross profit forecast.

- Revised gross profit forecast: Revised contract price minus (cost to date + cost to complete).

The following column-by-column explanation provides additional information for Sample 13, Work-in-Progress Report:

- Contract price: This is the contract price the customer has agreed to pay for the work or estimate of the projected price for contracts that are not a fixed price.

- Revised contract price: Contracts and budget prices inevitably get revised. This column represents the revised contract price.

- Cost to date: The cost to date for the project determined from the job cost reports for the project.

- Cost to complete: This is an estimate of the cost to complete the project. It is a re-estimate of the cost to complete and not a guess or mathematical calculation.

- Invoiced to date: The total invoiced to date.

- Billings received: The total payments received to date on contracts in progress.

- Billings due: The amount outstanding as a receivable on the contract. This is columns E (invoiced to date) minus F (billings received).

- Work in progress: This is a mathematical calculation based on the following formula of columns: (C=I) minus F (billings received).

- Profit earned to date: This is a mathematical calculation based on the following formula of the columns: (C/(C=D))*K.

- Original gross profit forecast: This is the gross profit you originally estimated for the project which would be the contract price minus the estimated cost for the project.

- Revised gross profit forecast: This is the revised gross profit for the project taking into account contract revisions and estimated cost to complete the project. The formula for this calculation of columns is: B minus C minus D.

Now that you have your work-in-progress report completed you can figure out the following:

- Work on hand: This is the amount of work and related gross profit that is outstanding as of the date of the report. This can now be calculated as: (sum of cost to complete) plus (sum of revised gross profit forecast) minus (sum of profit earned to date).

- Total accounts receivable: This is the total amount of outstanding invoices to be collected.

- Gross profit percentage for work completed on this report: (profit earned to date) ÷ (billed to date + work in progress) expressed as a percentage.

On projects that are in progress over a period of months you need to calculate what you should have invoiced versus what you did invoice. It is unlikely that you will invoice exactly what you should for the work completed to date for projects that are in progress. Therefore, you complete a contract summary at month end to determine in total if you have invoiced too much or not enough. The resulting number is referred to as "work in progress." If the number is positive, you have underbilled the project; if the number is negative you have overbilled the project. Work in progress will appear on your balance sheet as an asset if you have underbilled in total on all projects in progress and a liability if you have overbilled.

Depending on the number of contracts in progress, the contract summary is one or two pages which provide some very concise information. The following is what you're looking for when you are reviewing the contract summary report:

1. For each contract:

   - Look at the completion date. For example, the completion date is June and it's currently August. There is still a number in the cost to complete column, which may be a problem that needs to be looked into. You should be aware that there is a problem and you are monitoring the project and have an answer for anyone who may ask.

   - Compare the contract price to the revised contract price. Is this project growing in size or staying the same? If it is growing, you would expect the revised gross profit forecast to be growing as well.

   - Compare the cost to date to the cost to complete; this gives you an indication of how much work is left to do on the project.

   - Look at billed to date, billings received, billings due, and work in progress. Are there any trouble spots here? A positive work in progress means that there are costs incurred that have not been billed. Is there an issue with billings?

   - Work in progress in an ideal world would be zero. It would mean that every contract has been invoiced for all costs incurred and profit earned to date and that would be a very rare occurrence. You need to be aware that for every

Company name: *ABC CONSTRUCTION COMPANY*
Contract summary as at: *July 1, 20--*

Sample 13
Work-in-Progress Report

Project Description	A Contract Price	B Revised Contract Price	C Cost to Date	D Cost to Complete	E Invoiced to Date	F Billings Received	G Billings Due	H Work in Progress	I Profit Earned to Date	J Original Gross Profit Forecast	K Revised Gross Profit Forecast
Job #1001	10,000	10,000	1,000	6,981	1,200	–	1,200	53	253	2,000	2,019
Job #1002	20,000	25,000	10,000	9,201	12,000	6,000	6,000	1,020	3,020	5,000	5,799
Job #1003	30,000	30,000	20,000	2,256	24,000	15,000	9,000	2,959	6,959	6,000	7,744
Job #1004	40,000	45,000	30,000	4,852	38,000	30,000	8,000	735	8,735	9,000	10,148
Job #1005	50,000	55,000	10,000	34,256	15,000	2,000	13,000	2,572	2,428	10,000	10,744
Total	**150,000**	**165,000**	**71,000**	**57,546**	**90,200**	**53,000**	**37,200**	**2,195**	**21,395**	**32,000**	**36,454**

positive work-in-progress number, you have recorded and possibly paid for costs that have not been billed to the customer.

- Original gross profit forecast versus revised gross profit forecast. Which way is this project trending? There is no worse number than zero or a negative in this column. If it is negative, you are not only doing this job for free, you are actually taking money out of your own pocket and giving it to the customer. This is not what you expected on this project so is there anything you can do about it at this stage to turn this project around?

2. For all column totals:

- How does your work on hand look? Do you need more work, are you overloaded with work, or is work on hand just about right?

- How do total billings due look? This is the sum of all the money owed to you on all projects in progress. Is it manageable, are payments coming in slow, or is action needed?

- Is total work in progress positive or negative? A large positive number could represent a lot of unbilled costs and profit which is never good.

- How does your gross profit percentage look? Your annual budget should have predetermined a target gross profit percentage for all work to be completed this fiscal year; consider how reality is shaping up compared to the budget.

In reviewing all of the project data there is one critical variable and that is the estimated cost to complete. All of the other project data is either factual (e.g., job number), based on project data (e.g., contract or budget), the result of a mathematical formula (i.e., work in progress), and most critical of all, the cost to complete is an estimate. Therefore, of all of the project data and criteria the only item that is estimated is the cost to complete. If the cost-to-complete estimate is inaccurate, the entire project job-cost report is inaccurate and not worth the paper it's written on.

If the cost-to-complete estimates are not accurate and reliable, nine times out of ten they are estimated too low, not too high. Too high an estimate you may be able to live with, but an underestimation of project costs to complete could lead you into a false sense of security that the project is going along just fine, when in fact you are headed for a disaster. Like I said earlier, anyone can estimate the cost to complete when the project is 0 or 100 percent complete; it takes real skill to create an accurate and reliable cost-to-complete estimate when the project is in progress. If you can create accurate and reliable cost-to-complete estimates, you are on your way to making a lot of money in your business. If you can't create accurate and reliable cost-to-complete estimates, maybe you should consider another profession.

6. Asset Management

From day one in your business you are going to accumulate assets. How you manage your assets is critical to the success of your business. Your accountant can advise on how you should manage your assets per various classes for tax purposes. What I am referring to here is how you manage your assets to benefit the day-to-day operation of your business. Obviously you should only be accumulating assets that will provide benefits to your business; in the short and long term.

Besides your holdings in land and buildings, your business assets can typically be divided into the following categories:

- Small tools.

- Major equipment.

Small tools are easily identified if you establish a replacement cost level for your company and every tool acquired below this threshold is classified as a "small tool." For example, if you establish a threshold of $1,000, every tool you acquire with a replacement value of $1,000 or less will be classified as a small tool.

"Major equipment" is everything else with a replacement value of more than $1,000. This includes major shop equipment, vehicles, mobile equipment, specialized field equipment, etc. The decision to purchase major equipment needs to be made by a process, not just on a whim that you need something new. Why? The answer is that you need the piece of equipment in order to achieve Faster, Cheaper, Better (FCB) results on your projects.

Keep in mind FCB as you analyze the piece of equipment and whether or not you should acquire it for your business. You are the only one who can determine the benefits and make the best decision for your company. With all major equipment there are options, which can double the cost; therefore, all of this must be taken into consideration when applying FCB principles to your decision. For example, you can walk into the showroom of a dealership and look at a very nice $20,000 truck, but by the time you leave you have spent $40,000 with all the extras the salesperson offers you. The same thing can happen with every purchase of major equipment.

The next decision is: How do you plan on paying for your purchase? Here are your options:

- Cash: Paying in cash uses working capital. You'll need to consider whether or not the business can afford to have working capital tied up in major equipment assets.

- Finance: Typical options are through your bank, or vendor financing, which can be very competitive.

- Lease: Businesses today will lease you anything you want under a number of term options. If you are not careful, you can end up with an abundance of leases and the resulting long-term liability that leases bind you to. Have your bookkeeper carefully manage lease commitments by creating a lease commitment report. This will keep you abreast of lease termination dates, optional or mandatory buyout terms, and other commitments under the lease. To lease or to buy is a decision best made after consulting with your accountant.

- Rent: Do you really need to acquire an asset or is renting a viable option?

Now that you have made a decision to acquire a piece of major equipment, you will need to consider maintenance and service. The cost of purchasing major equipment is only part of the story. You have to look at all costs throughout the life of the equipment.

Don't forget disposal costs, because at the end of the useful life of the equipment you will have to dispose of it. Every self-employed entrepreneur who has retired believes that all the equipment he or she has acquired over the years is worth hundreds of thousands of dollars when in fact every potential purchaser is typically prepared to pay pennies on the dollar for the equipment. This is not always true when it comes to specialized equipment; however, it is almost always true when it comes to common equipment. Be prepared for this day so you won't be shocked. This bit of reality has to be taken into consideration when acquiring major equipment.

Costs related to small tools and major equipment should be allocated to the projects where the tools and equipment are being used. Small tools can best be managed by applying a percentage allocation to a project. For example, a percentage of your labor costs will be used as an allocation for small tools. Major equipment should be allocated to projects based on utilization as if you were renting the equipment to the project. Obviously, all of these costs need to be taken into consideration when completing your cost estimate for the project. A surefire way of being the lowest bidder on a project is to not allocate any equipment costs to the project: Do this at your own peril!

From an accounting point of view all capital assets are depreciated; meaning that their value goes down over time. Depreciation rates vary from asset class to asset class. Land typically doesn't depreciate. Allowance for depreciation per asset class is a function that can be handled in your chosen accounting program.

7. Financial Reporting

Every accounting program on the market will provide you with a range of reports; in fact, too many to read or consider. In business you need clear and concise information that is accurate and reliable. You don't want to miss anything but summary reports are much easier to read and absorb than multipage reports. You have to remember that financial reports are produced for your benefit and the information in the reports is designed to help you manage your business better: To be a Faster, Cheaper, Better company.

You can't let the abundance of reports overwhelm you or unnecessarily tie you to your desk. Work with your bookkeeper and/or accountant to create reports that are clear and concise and that will provide you with the most benefit. Remember, if you spot an issue, or there is a concern, you can ask for additional information of which there will be lots available. The following are the key reports you do need to understand:

- Monthly financial statements.

- Monthly financial summaries which can include an abundance of summary information, for example:
  - Sales summaries.
  - Work-in-progress reports.
  - Marketing summaries.
  - Accounts receivable.
  - Accounts payable.
  - Personnel (e.g., number of employees, new hires, and layoffs).
- Job cost reports prepared for each project.
- Summary job cost report.
- Aged accounts receivable lists.
- Aged accounts payable lists.

8. Cash Flow

Cash flow is a projection of how funds are going to flow through your company or bank account over a period of time, typically for a month, but could be for any specified period of time and projected forward for up to a year or more.

Each month, you are going to start off with some money in the bank. During the month you are going to have withdrawals for job costs and expenses as well as deposits when you receive payments from customers. At the end of the month you will have a new bank balance. What happens throughout the month with withdrawals and deposits defines your cash flow.

Sample 14 illustrates accounts receivable collected on time and Sample 15 shows a situation in which the receivables were not collected on time. Please note the extreme difference. Receivables must be collected on time in order for your business to function.

A cash-flow statement will provide you with other information as well including the need for working capital, the need for an arranged line of credit at the bank, and when suppliers need to be paid.

Sample 14
Cash-Flow Statement with All Accounts Receivable Collected on Time

Description/Month	Jan	Feb	Mar	Apr	May	Jun	Jul	Aug	Sept	Oct	Nov	Dec
Opening Bank Balance	50,000	55,000	60,000	65,000	70,000	75,000	80,000	85,000	90,000	95,000	100,000	105,000
Withdrawals for Wages	30,000	30,000	30,000	30,000	30,000	30,000	30,000	30,000	30,000	30,000	30,000	30,000
Withdrawals for Other Project Costs	50,000	50,000	50,000	50,000	50,000	50,000	50,000	50,000	50,000	50,000	50,000	50,000
Withdrawals for Expenses	10,000	10,000	10,000	10,000	10,000	10,000	10,000	10,000	10,000	10,000	10,000	10,000
Withdrawals for Mortgages and Loans	5,000	5,000	5,000	5,000	5,000	5,000	5,000	5,000	5,000	5,000	5,000	5,000
Deposits from Customer Sales	100,000	100,000	100,000	100,000	100,000	100,000	100,000	100,000	100,000	100,000	100,000	100,000
Closing Bank Balance	**55,000**	**60,000**	**65,000**	**70,000**	**75,000**	**80,000**	**85,000**	**90,000**	**95,000**	**100,000**	**105,000**	**110,000**

The banker is happy because your account has a positive balance each and every month because your receivables are collected on time each month.

Sample 15
Cash-Flow Statement with Some Accounts Receivable Not Collected on Time

Description/Month	Jan	Feb	Mar	Apr	May	Jun	Jul	Aug	Sept	Oct	Nov	Dec
Opening Bank Balance	50,000	55,000	50,000	35,000	10,000	-25,000	-70,000	-115,000	-135,000	-105,000	-75,000	-20,000
Withdrawals for Wages	30,000	30,000	30,000	30,000	30,000	30,000	30,000	30,000	30,000	30,000	30,000	30,000
Withdrawals for Other Project Costs	50,000	50,000	50,000	50,000	50,000	50,000	50,000	50,000	50,000	50,000	50,000	50,000
Withdrawals for Expenses	10,000	10,000	10,000	10,000	10,000	10,000	10,000	10,000	10,000	10,000	10,000	10,000
Withdrawals for Mortgages and Loans	5,000	5,000	5,000	5,000	5,000	5,000	5,000	5,000	5,000	5,000	5,000	5,000
Deposits from Customer Sales	100,000	90,000	80,000	70,000	60,000	50,000	50,000	75,000	125,000	125,000	150,000	100,000
Closing Bank Balance	**55,000**	**50,000**	**35,000**	**10,000**	**-25,000**	**-70,000**	**-115,000**	**-135,000**	**-105,000**	**-75,000**	**-20,000**	**-15,000**

The banker is unhappy because you have not collected your receivables on time and your account is overdrawn.

In this scenario, if the bank will not accommodate your overdraft, you won't be able to pay your suppliers and meet other commitments; your business will be in trouble.

Bottom Line: You must collect your receivables on time.

10
Risks

Everything we do in life involves risk. All risks cannot be eliminated. Some risks can be avoided, while others cannot be avoided but can be managed.

Most of us go through our day-to-day lives not thinking too much about risk. Many people eliminate risks in life by not pursuing a career as a tightrope walker or race car driver. Most of us avoid risks that cannot be eliminated; for example, we can't eliminate the risks of walking down the street, but we can avoid the risk of getting run over by crossing at a marked crosswalk. Risks that cannot be avoided can be managed such as wearing your seatbelt when you drive your vehicle.

Risks in business are similar to risks in life. The difference between everyday life risks and business risks is that we have a lifetime of experience on how to identify risks in life; but if you are new to business, you don't have any experience on how to identify business risks. A business risk that isn't identified cannot be eliminated, avoided, or managed; it will be waiting there to poke up its ugly head and bite you in the butt when you least expect it! A risk that is identified can possibly be eliminated, avoided, or managed.

1. Identify the Risks

Your job is to identify risks in your business, and more specifically to identify risks on projects that you are considering undertaking, then determine how to deal with the identified risks. This is important to remember: *Risks in business that are not identified cannot be eliminated, avoided, or managed.*

This is what you need to consider when you have identified the risk:

- Can the risk be eliminated? If so, develop a plan to eliminate it.

- Can the risk be avoided? If so, develop a plan to avoid it.

- Can the risk be managed? If so, develop a plan to manage it.

The following sections identify the most common risks to business in the selling it, building it for less than you sold it, and accounting for it phases. This is not an exhaustive list. The objective of this chapter is to teach you how to identify the most important risks so you can eliminate, avoid, or manage them. These are the consequences of not eliminating, avoiding, or managing risk:

- Not meeting your Customer's Project Objectives.

- Not meeting Faster, Cheaper, Better project objectives.

- Financial losses.

- Financial disaster.

- "Small-business hell."

2. "Selling It" Risks

The following sections will help you identify the "selling it" risks. They will give you guidance on whether or not to eliminate, avoid, or manage the risks.

2.1 Misunderstanding project objectives

Eliminate this risk: Do a thorough job of understanding and documenting your Customer's Project Objectives on each and every project. You will find very quickly and with experience that you will be able to lead the understanding and documentation process with your customer, and I can assure you that this will put you into a preferred position on the project with your customer.

2.2 Customer misunderstandings about objectives and pricing

Eliminate this risk: Do a good job of documenting your Customer's Project Objectives and follow up with clear and concise pricing information.

2.3 Underestimating the cost of a project

Manage this risk: This risk cannot be eliminated or avoided in its entirety without making your bid totally uncompetitive. Use accurate and reliable historical job cost records and your project experience to ensure that you prepare an accurate and reliable cost for the project.

2.4 Bidding too low on a project

Avoid this pitfall: Assuming you have prepared an accurate and reliable job cost estimate, the risk of bidding too low for a project remains in your hands as to what is a fair markup for the project. You want to be competitive but you have to make a fair and reasonable profit. If your competitors want to do the project for no profit, let them.

2.5 Lack of understanding of a project's complexity and unforeseen conditions

Eliminate this risk: You have to take the time and use your experience to ensure you understand the complexity of the project and have the vision to foresee conditions. If you can't eliminate or avoid the risk, manage it by identifying the risk in your project objectives and put in conditions that ensure that you will not be damaged or hurt if the risk occurs. For example, if a project has a very tight schedule and weather is a risk, put into your conditions that the schedule will be adjusted for production days lost or affected due to weather.

Dependence on other contractors is almost always an issue, so when contractors fail to meet the scheduled objectives, be sure to include a condition that will adjust the schedule for situations like this.

2.6 Lack of resources to undertake your project commitments

Manage this risk: On any given project you are committing to provide all of the resources to complete the project. At this stage you need to know that the required resources will be available when required. Labor shortages and material delivery delays can all have an extremely adverse effect on a project. Unfortunately this risk cannot be totally eliminated or avoided, so you have to manage it.

During the selling phase, investigate the availability of required resources such as labor, materials, subcontractors, and accommodation for site personnel on out-of-town projects. Potential resource shortages identified at this stage can be managed and/or accommodated within the project estimate and/or conditions.

2.7 Issues with subcontractors and suppliers

Eliminate this risk: The best way to avoid this risk is to only use subcontractors and suppliers that you know will meet all of the project objectives. Surround yourself with good suppliers and subcontractors. One bad subcontractor or supplier could put the entire project off the rails. This risk must be eliminated. If you are contemplating using subcontractors or suppliers with whom you are not familiar, check them out before you commit to using them.

2.8 Unscrupulous customers

Eliminate this risk: Believe it or not there are unscrupulous customers out there. They could be general contractors, developers, end users, or homeowners. You don't want to do work for these types of customers. Check out your potential customers and make sure they are upstanding, creditworthy, and someone with whom you want to do business. If you have any doubts, say thanks and pass on the job.

2.9 Poor relationship with the customer

Eliminate this risk: You must believe that you can develop a good relationship with your customer. If you don't believe you can develop a good relationship, you should pass on the project. You need to focus on customers you believe will appreciate the unique and extraordinary approach that you will bring to their project. Customers who can't see beyond the lowest price are going to have a tough time appreciating your commitment to Faster, Cheaper, Better. Price is extremely important, but there is a lot more to a project than a low price. Your best customers will recognize this; these are the customers you need to focus on, and eliminate all the rest.

2.10 Lack of vision

Eliminate this risk: You need to have a vision for the project you are pursuing. You need to envision scheduling risks, cost risks, and quality risks. You never want to say to yourself: "I never thought of that." You need to eliminate this risk to the best of your ability by using your experience to envision potential risks on the project and then take appropriate action.

3. "Building It for Less Than You Sold It" Risks

The following sections will help you identify the "building it for less than you sold it" risks. They will give you guidance on whether or not to eliminate, avoid, or manage the risks.

3.1 Not meeting your Customer's Project Objectives

Manage this risk: This is one of the biggest potential risks of all. The customer could have 100 project objectives and if you fail to meet just one of them, the project could be a disaster. Meeting your Customer's Project Objectives doesn't mean meeting *some* of the objectives, it means meeting *all* of your Customer's Project Objectives. For example, a baker prepared the biggest and nicest wedding cake of his career in which he met all of the bride's objectives except for the schedule; he delivered the cake the Monday after the wedding. The fact that he met 99 out of 100 objectives wasn't good enough. The customer needed all of her objectives met.

Manage this risk during the selling stage so that all of the Customer's Project Objectives are identified and documented. At this stage it is the project manager's responsibility to meet all of the defined objectives.

3.2 Project mismanagement

Eliminate this risk: It is project *management* not project *mismanagement*. Projects can be mismanaged for any number of reasons but the reasons are only excuses. When it comes to project management, don't accept excuses, only accept results. Eliminate this risk by making best project management practices in your business mandatory and accept nothing less under any circumstances.

3.3 Not building the project Faster, Cheaper, Better

Eliminate this risk: You are committing to an overall Faster, Cheaper, Better job compared to your competitors. Eliminate the risk of not meeting the objectives of Faster, Cheaper, Better by adopting this policy throughout your company. Ensure all your employees are trained in Faster, Cheaper, Better practices and, above all, manage your projects using these three objectives.

3.4 Not building it for less than you sold it

Eliminate this risk: Not making a reasonable profit should be a criminal offence in our industry. You are in business to make money not to lose money. Everything you do from the minute you start work in the morning to the time you quit for the day has to focus on making a reasonable profit on each and every project.

3.5 Inaccurate and unreliable cost-to-complete estimates

Eliminate this risk: This is one of the greatest risks to a project. An inaccurate and unreliable cost-to-complete estimate on a project could send the entire project off the rails. You may believe you are on track to making your estimated profit on a project, but if in fact you are destined to lose a substantial amount of money, then you are totally misguided. Only an accurate and reliable cost-to-complete estimate can provide you with the information you need in order to effectively manage the project to ensure the project meets its objectives. Eliminate this risk by ensuring the project manager has the skills, abilities, vision, knowledge, and facts in order to prepare accurate and reliable cost-to-complete estimates. This is one of the most important management tools you can have.

4. "Accounting for It" Risks

The following sections will help you identify the "accounting for it" risks. They will give you guidance on whether or not to eliminate, avoid, or manage the risks.

4.1 Under capitalization

Eliminate this risk: If you are undercapitalized and have overextended yourself, even though you may be making a profit on your projects, you could be putting your company at risk. If you have all of your capital tied up in accounts receivable and no funds available to make payroll, you are going to be in a lot of trouble.

Eliminate this risk by seeking professional advice to determine capitalization requirements for your business and then maintain the required capital in your business. Don't take on projects that have the potential of over utilizing your available capital.

4.2 Not getting paid by your customer on schedule

Eliminate this risk: You can be doing everything else right but if your customer doesn't pay you on time, you are not going to be able to fulfill your commitments. Your bank is not going to lend you any money against overdue receivables.

This risk must be eliminated by ensuring invoices are issued accurately and on time in accordance with the project terms and conditions, and you must insist that your customer pay you on schedule. If, for any reason beyond your control, your customer doesn't or can't pay you on schedule, you must be prepared to take appropriate and immediate action.

4.3 The customer has financial difficulties

Eliminate this risk: This is a call you never want to get. "We are sorry, but we just went broke and you are not going to get paid." Believe me, this happens.

This risk must be eliminated at the "selling it" phase to ensure that you are offering your services only to customers who are financially stable with the ability to complete the project even if they face major challenges on their end. For every dollar you don't collect on an account receivable you have to do about $20 in business just to get back to even. Not a good prospect. You are fulfilling your obligations on the project and you deserve to get paid; that is the deal and any other alternative is not acceptable.

4.4 Personnel problems

Manage this risk: Human resource (HR) matters can be infinite in number; for example, alcohol and drug issues, family problems, poor performance, lack of initiative, poor training, unsafe work practices, insubordination, and lack of respect. This list can go on and on.

Manage this risk by hiring first-class people. There is an old saying that first-class people hire first-class people and second-class people hire third-class people. Go first class! Employ great HR practices, and ensure you are hiring the best people for the job. In today's economy you are likely going to pay a poor employee about the same as a good employee, so you may as well hire the best from the get go.

4.5 Inaccurate and unreliable job-cost reporting

Eliminate this risk: Applying an accurate and reliable cost-to-complete estimate to an inaccurate and unreliable job cost report will result in disastrous misinformation. Accounting and bookkeeping must produce accurate and reliable information that responsible personnel and project managers can rely on and trust. Consistent misinformation from the bookkeeper will skew the entire organization and head the business towards disaster. Eliminate this risk by employing the best skills in bookkeeping and accounting and demand accurate and reliable information.

11
Suppliers

Suppliers, wholesalers, jobbers, and distributors are just a few of the names we use for our material and equipment providers. Some of the names are unique to specific trades but for sake of clarity I will refer to them all collectively as "suppliers" and everything provided through the suppliers as "material," even though the supply may go beyond material to include equipment, tools, consumables, and other project requirements.

Unless you are strictly a labor broker, suppliers will be an integral part of your business. As contractors and service providers, the reselling of materials is a major part of our business. Labor and materials make up the majority of costs on a project. For many businesses the cost of materials can exceed the cost of labor.

In the absence of material there is nothing you can do. You can have all of the other resources accounted for and in place but if you don't have the materials you need, where and when they are required, your productivity on the project will grind to a halt. Not a great way to achieve Faster, Cheaper, Better.

Your suppliers are in business to make money just like you are. You are their customer and, much like in your business, their objective is to meet your project objectives. For the most part your supplier's role may be less complex than the role you play on the project in that the supplier is typically "supply only," but without your supplier meeting its commitments you won't be able to meet your Customer's Project Objectives. Your supplier wants to meet the objectives you have defined. The supplier wants you to be a happy, repeat customer and the best way it can accomplish that is to meet your objectives.

These are the typical objectives that you define for your suppliers:

- Meeting the scheduled delivery date.

- Competitive pricing.

- Quality materials and service.

What else could you ask for? You can summarize these supplier objectives as: schedule, price, and quality. Do these objectives look vaguely familiar to Faster, Cheaper, Better? That's right. You want the same thing from your suppliers as you have committed to providing to your customer: Faster, Cheaper, Better. If your supplier's commitments to you are in line with your commitments to your customer, and your supplier meets all of its defined objectives, then that is a major step towards helping you meet your Faster, Cheaper, Better objectives.

We've hammered away throughout the book about identifying and documenting your Customers' Project Objectives. If their objectives aren't identified and documented then there is a chance that they won't be met. This applies to your suppliers, as well. You and your supplier need to communicate so that your supplier can identify and document your objectives. Failing that, how can you expect your supplier to meet your objectives?

How well do you understand your supplier's business? Most suppliers are just that — suppliers. They are not manufactures although they may provide a range of supplementary services. Therefore, your supplier buys supplies, equipment, tools, and products from manufacturers or major distributors and resells these products to you. Most contractors are too small to deal directly with manufacturers and factories so the supplier's role is key as the go-between for you, the contractor, and the multitude of manufacturers that build the materials and equipment that you need for your projects.

Imagine the number and quantity of materials it takes to put together one project. Even a small project may take hundreds of parts to complete. Major projects could have hundreds of thousands of parts, if not millions. Each part has to be purchased, shipped to the site, managed on the site, and installed. It is absolutely amazing when you think of all the components of a major project. From the smallest nuts and bolts to major steel girders; from dozens of kinds of nails to a multitude of sizes and lengths of lumber; from drywall to plaster; from light switches to toilets; from pipe to concrete. The list is infinitely long. If you are missing one properly sized nut and bolt, a portion of the project could come to a halt.

This should give you a better idea of just how important your suppliers are and the importance of your relationship with your suppliers. Behind the counter at your suppliers' place are representatives with knowledge about hundreds of thousands of parts, and you need these representatives to help wade through the intense maze to get you exactly what you want, on schedule, and at a competitive price. Your suppliers and their representatives have no problem with this challenge. This is their business; this is what they do. They should be doing their business in the same professional manner as you are managing your business.

Looking at the industry from all your suppliers' points of view, what do they want in their relationship with you? To do a lot of business with you would be the obvious answer. However, they want more than that. They want the same things in their business relationship with you as you want with your customers. They want to have a good relationship with you as a customer; they want to meet the objectives you have laid down for them; they want to profit from their relationship with you; and they want to be paid in accordance with the terms and conditions of their sales agreements with you. If all of those things happen, you've created a win-win situation between you and your supplier. A win-win relationship with suppliers will go a long way towards helping you meet your project objectives for your customers.

The supply chain in our industry is not that long. It basically starts with manufacturers, then suppliers, then contractors, and then the end user. If there is any break in the chain, the end user is the ultimate loser.

Most suppliers' corporate structures are multi-branch and located throughout their service area. Their service areas could be local, state, provincial, or multi-state or multi-province. Most suppliers work on tight margins so the more buying power they have, the better prices they can offer to their customers. Quality service, quality products, and reliable delivery are the mantra of most suppliers; hence, Faster, Cheaper, Better. Because of their corporate structures, most suppliers are larger companies that may be independently owned or they may be part of a multinational organization or public company.

1. Supplier Credit

Many suppliers have policies in place that cover most aspects of their businesses. One of these policies is credit. Your supplier's credit policy will dictate the amount of credit your supplier is willing to grant you and the terms and conditions of that credit. Your supplier typically has limited ability to secure its credit position other than seeking personal guarantees and its ability to impose a builder's lien if it doesn't get paid.

Since your suppliers are one or two steps removed from the projects and end users, they aren't in an enviable position when it comes to the priority ranking of creditors. Your suppliers are all well aware of their positions in this regard and the risk they take in granting credit. Obviously, your suppliers have a vested interest in the way you manage your business and in your success. If you are running a well-managed and profitable business, your suppliers are well assured that they are going to be paid on time. If you read, understand, and implement the business practices in this book, you are going to have a well-managed and profitable business. Therefore, your suppliers have a vested interest in you applying the business practices of Faster, Cheaper, Better.

Suppliers, collectively, write off millions of dollars in bad debts every year. Behind every bad debt is an unfortunate story where something has gone wrong. This is what this book is all about — preventing things from going wrong.

Being a good customer for your suppliers means you are going to be the beneficiary of preferred pricing, preferred service, and quality supplies. However, if you have a deteriorated relationship with a supplier, all of these benefits go south and your business will be affected. This means from day one in your business, one of your primary business goals must be to maintain good relationships with your suppliers and this always starts with you paying your suppliers on time in accordance with their payment terms. If you miss payments, always pay late, and put your suppliers at risk of not getting paid, you will face the brunt of an organization that no longer wants to do business with you. Losing good suppliers is going to make your life very difficult when it comes to meeting your Customer's Project Objectives.

Your suppliers are your partners in ensuring you can meet your objectives. Similar to any good partnership, there must be respect, understanding, commitment, and communication, which are all very valuable components in a good, long-lasting relationship. Make it a priority to have a great relationship with your suppliers and you will derive the benefits, every day, in your business.

12

It's Time to Make Some Money!

If you think profit is a bad word, then you have just wasted time reading the first eleven chapters of this book. Profit is not a bad word; profit is the lifeblood of every for-profit business. A business is in business to make a profit — not to lose money, not to break even, but to make a profit.

How much profit should you make? Personally, I subscribe to making a fair and reasonable profit on each and every project. In my opinion, greed is not a good business trait to have. Meager profit says: "Why are you bothering to be in business?" A fair and reasonable profit on each and every project will ensure the success of your business, and, more important, will be the driving force behind your commitment to make your business a success.

In order to figure out what a fair and reasonable profit is, research other businesses in your field and find out how much money they are making. Does five or ten cents on every dollar of business seem to be the average? For example, if you do $100,000 in business, you should expect a minimum profit of $5,000, and potentially up to $10,000. If you do $1 million of business annually, you should expect a minimum profit of $50,000, but a $100,000 profit would be much better. These levels of profit are not greedy; they are fair and reasonable profit expectations.

The profit I am referring to here is net profit before taxes but after all costs of sales and expenses are accounted for including payment of wages (or an allowance for) to the owner. Artificially boosting profits by not paying yourself a reasonable wage is a false economy. There are things you may want to do for accounting and tax purposes, but at the end of the day your net profit before taxes must be calculated after you have allowed for a reasonable wage for the owner. For example, as the sole owner of your business, your sales are $1 million per year so you might pay yourself a salary of $75,000 per year. You should earn a profit of between $50,000 and $100,000 for the year before an allowance for taxes. Now that is incentive!

How can you justify earning this kind of money? With your salary and your profit for the year described above you have effectively earned between $125,000 and $175,000. Does this sound unreasonable to you? All of your salary is your salary; if you weren't doing the job in your company you would have to hire someone at $75,000 to do the job. Your profit is what you have earned in your business, a profit that represents a return on investment and a return on the business enterprise. By not paying yourself a fair wage, you are living in a false economy. If your company does not earn a fair and reasonable profit for the year, you are putting the company in jeopardy and into a position in which the company will not be able to prosper and grow.

As stated previously, profit is the lifeblood of any for-profit enterprise. Without profit or with only a meager profit, an enterprise cannot grow and prosper.

1. What Happens to the Profits in Your Company?

In the early stages of your business you'll likely want to retain the profits in the business to build retained earnings, reduce debt, and increase working capital. This is one more reason why you want to pay yourself a reasonable salary. You and your family can live off of your salary and the profit can be applied to the full benefit of the business.

Of course, a reasonable annual dividend or bonus paid to yourself for your extraordinary efforts throughout the year would certainly seem reasonable. When your family benefits from the profits in your business, they will better appreciate the "beyond the call of duty" efforts that you put into your business and they will realize they are worthwhile after all.

Ideally, business growth should be fuelled by retained earnings and not the accumulation of more debt. Let's say that your business is doing $1 million a year in business and your business has $100,000 of invested working capital and $100,000 line of credit. You would like to grow your business to $2 million a year in business, so you should increase your working capital to $200,000; you do this by building up working capital by retaining your after-tax earnings in your company. You will find this method a lot easier than trying to borrow the $100,000 to grow your business. Growth by retained earnings is the best way to grow your business.

What happens over a period of time when you are no longer growing your business and your business has more than adequate working capital? What do you do with your profits? You should seek the advice of a professional accountant or an investment advisor. You have reached the pinnacle of success and you are now building some very serious net worth.

Am I telling you that your business, if successful, has the ability to make you wealthy? Yes, I am. You may have never had the vision of being wealthy and here you are, after a number of years of running your own business, finding yourself in a position of wealth. Amazing? No! Deserved? Yes!

Have you heard of the 80/20 rule? This rule can be applied to so many things in life and in business. I hold to the theory that 80 percent of the profits made in our industry are earned by 20 percent of the companies. This may be a stretch, but it indicates that 80 percent of the companies in our industry are underperforming and not making the profit that they should. However, the 20 percent of companies that are earning 80 percent of the profits in our industry are the stability of our industry, the most viable, the best run, and the most successful. Which group would you like to be in? If your company fits the profile, your company is in the elite 20 percent of companies in our industry who consistently earn profits in excess of 5 percent of sales each and every year. A very enviable position to be in! To those companies in the 80 percent group, it's definitely time to reread *Faster, Cheaper, Better* and put into action the many good business practices that are advocated throughout the book, and work up to reasonable profit expectations to join the elite 20 percent group.

Conclusion

Is Faster, Cheaper, Better idealism or believable? Is Faster, Cheaper, Better pure speculation or achievable? Is Faster, Cheaper, Better unrealistic or realistic? Is Faster, Cheaper, Better wishful thinking or within your power?

Fastest, cheapest, best is idealism, pure speculation, unrealistic, and wishful thinking.

Faster, Cheaper, Better is believable, achievable, realistic, and within your power!

- That is why it's *Faster* not fastest or faster when compared to all of your competitors.

- That is why it's *Cheaper* not cheapest or cheaper when compared to all of your competitors.

- That is why it's *Better* not best or better when compared to all of your competitors.

When combined into a believable, achievable, realistic, and within your power business culture, you will be the preferred contractor on every job you approach, the most successful contractor on every job you work, the most profitable contractor year after year, and the contractor most looked up to in your industry. What else could you ask for in business?

Faster, Cheaper, Better: A culture for your business and one you can foster within your company. The Faster, Cheaper, Better ways can permeate your business from the top all the way to the bottom and make your business a success beyond your wildest dreams.

Download Kit

Please type the URL you see in the box below into your web browser to access and download the kit.

```
www.self-counsel.com/updates/fastcheapbetter/14kit.htm
```

The kit includes forms and resources to help you with your business:

- Invoice and purchase order templates.

- Entrepreneur assessment quizzes.

- Job cost estimate and report templates.

- Project proposal and cash flow projection worksheets.

- — And more!